Born of Violence
Triumph Over Tragedy: Living Out God's Purpose

a memoir

KIMYA MOTLEY

Published by: Kimya Motley, LLC

Cover Design by: WJ Enterprises/
Photo Credit: SLV Photo

Dear Reader,

This memoir details the events that unfolded before, during, and after my marriage. There are some events told that highlight aspects of my childhood from the age of five through my teen years, early adulthood, and the road of abuse which led to that fateful day on September 20th and beyond.

I have been faithful to my memory; however, the recollections of the people involved in my story may be different from my memories. Due to the sensitive nature of some of the events depicted, some of the names and characteristics of people have been changed to protect all parties involved.

No portion of this book has been written to harm any of the people involved. It has been written to bring healing and hope to people that are ready to bounce back from their own personal challenges.

In referring to the abuser in this book, I have chosen to use the words He, Him, Or His and the words She or Her in reference to the victim. While I acknowledge that men are abused in relationships, statistically, women are abused more frequently and report the crime at a much higher rate.

Abuse is real; therefore, I describe the reality of violence in the pages of this memoir which involve sex, profanity, physical violence and drug use, which may trigger memories or feelings in you. Continue reading and I promise that you will see God in these pages and He will give you the strength to turn your tragedies into triumph!

Love, Kimya

Dedication

Father God, you are my ride or die, shoulder to lean on, comforter, Father Jehovah Jireh, Nissi, Ropha, Shalom, and best friend. I am in awe of you and your love, grace, and mercy toward me. You loved me when I didn't love myself. You chose me when I wasn't worthy. Thanks for always being there!

Mommy, thank you for loving me unconditionally. You showed me the true meaning of strength through adversity. You always encouraged me, always loved me, and always accepted me. I promise to always bring our family honor and make you proud of me. I love you!

Daddy, thank you for the good times and the bad times. I will carry with me the memories of plane building, candle making, cookie baking, painting lessons, and the times I used to curl up on your back and go to sleep. I smile whenever I think of you. Even though you hurt us at times, I now know that you did what you knew how to do; although it was wrong, I forgive you. It is through you that God gave me the gift of forgiveness. I love you!

My son, Theron, you've taught me how to love unconditionally, the power of fighting for the people I love, and patience under fire. You are such a strong, intelligent, handsome, and caring young man.

My daughter, Corinne, your strength and obstinate determination give a new definition to the saying "when pigs fly." You have taught me to believe in miracles again. Your incredible strength always makes me stronger. I can't be a weakling because my daughter taught me better than that.

Theron and Corinne, you have defied all the odds, silenced all the critics, fought many battles, and won. We still have a lot of battles to fight, but if God is for us, who dares to stand against us? You just don't know how much you two are the wind beneath my wings. I love you both so much!

My big "seester," Sandy, thank you for always having my back. You were "Mommy," sister, and friend when I needed you to be. You helped me raise Theron and Corinne, and I couldn't have done it without you. I am so glad that we get to go through life together.

Courtney, you make me one proud auntie! I am so proud to see how mature and creative you are. I love you!

Andria, Rayna, Tosha, Shuron, Kelly, Nichelle, Nicole, and Patrice you are my best friends on the entire planet. What can I say about you that wouldn't require a whole book dedicated to each of you just to say how truly remarkable you are and how vital you are to my life (which is why I am putting you all in this one all inclusive, yet loving, and appreciative paragraph together)?

From being my prayer partners, ride or die chicks (or dude), armor bearers, midwives, psychologists, ready to throw a brick in a minute squad, vacation givers, encouragement when I had nothing left, sisters from another mister, brother from another mother, child care providers, village to help me raise Theron and Corinne, movie and dinner dates, exercise companions, beauty consultants, philanthropists, undying givers of a shoulder to lean and cry on, and—most of all—BEST friends that a woman could ever ask for. I love you to pieces and back together again (and that's better than what happened to Humpty Dumpty).

Kim, Erica (Shawn), and Shadonna, you three are my cousins, but you know you mean so much more to me than that. I am proud to call you sisters and friends. From the time we were younger until this very moment, thank you for always being there for me.

Aunts Reesa, Denise, Nora, Annie Pearl, Sue, Pattie, Betty Jean and Net, you have all shaped me into the woman that I am today. Besides my grandmothers, you helped me to form my relationship with God, and you've shown me what class, dignity, and grace look like. Thank you for your example. You've given me so much to strive for. You are true Proverbs 31 women.

Betty Leslie, Dora Smith, and Emily Motley, thank you for being there for me as a mother would. Your strength, discipline, love, time, and FOOD mean the world to me! I love you to the moon and back.

The prayer team, board members, FOCUS team, ELITE team and my young ladies of ELITE, Haven of Light Teens (TOLI) and Teen Talks Team, you all make what I do possible. I am so thankful to have you all walk this journey of life with me.

Table of Contents

Acknowledgements

Thank you to:

Margaret Stiggers, for sitting by Corinne's side and never leaving her when she was hospitalized for those weeks. I would not have been able to heal properly without your help and support and neither would she. You are an outstanding grandma and you mean the world to all of us.

Pastor Lee Johnson, thank you for that one intense debate at the kitchen table which caused me to think differently about my life, made me realize that freeing people from domestic violence was my calling from birth, and was the inspiration for the title of this book.

My amazing editor, Sarah Fox. You are not only funny and empathetic which made this process much easier, but you were very detail-oriented and inquisitive. I needed all of that to produce my magnum opus. Everyone needs to run out to book you now!

Wendy Davis, Nicole Johnson, Denise Motley, Angela Nichols, thank you for being my beta readers and giving me honest feedback. You gave me things to think about and reconsider. Your help and your friendship are important to me.

Andrea Dobbs, thank you for participating in my Facebook survey and helping me develop the amazing subtitle for this book!

Jackie Legare, Kiska Lyons Alvinette Maultsby, and parents of the students I have taught, thanks for bringing me journals as gifts over the years for my endless writing pleasure. Many of my high and low points in the days, weeks, and months after the shooting were captured on the pages of your gifts to me.

Kendrick Cheely and Clovis Samuels, thank you for being the FIRST men after the shooting to show me that strong, young, black men still believe in God and try to truly follow HIS will for their lives. I needed to see that at a time when I felt that there were no men capable of love! You always thought I was put in your lives to help you. You have no idea how much your example has helped me

Dr. Vernon Henderson and Dr. Joshua Chern without God using your awesome gifts, Corinne and I would not be here. Thank you for your dedication and true passion for people.

Valerie Mooney, Michael Lederman, and Tracey Dillon thank you for being there for us in the weeks after the shooting. You all went above and beyond for my family and me.

Amanda Pilgrim, thank you for all of our late-night phone calls and early morning conversations. You were more than an investigator on my case. I thank you for helping me grow emotionally and mentally in the weeks and months after the shooting. You are truly an example of what it means "to protect and serve."

Richard Read, your intelligence, strength, and compassion are remarkable. God used you to be my words when I couldn't speak and my legs when I couldn't stand. More importantly, your dedication to this case and my family helped me to find my voice and gave me the determination to want to be a voice for the voiceless – just like you.

Pastors Eric W. Lee and Jermaine T. Johnson, thank you both for allowing God to use you in a mighty way in my life. Pastor Lee, you and the Springfield family gave my family love and support at a time when we needed it the most – and you didn't even know us. Pastor Johnson, taking the time to mentor me in the beginning of my ministry helped me to build HOLI on a firm foundation!

You both called out the leader in me and pushed me into speaking publicly and church leadership when I didn't believe in myself and my purpose.

Wykeitha Patillar, Gretchen Bailey, Keisha Russell and Lynn Andrews, thank you for your prayers, talks, financial support, laughter, and for being my personal chauffeurs (Kiki and Gretchen) when I couldn't get around to take care of my baby. Love you all very much!

Mattie Russell and Shirley Williams thank you for being my "bonus" aunts. You all fed us when we didn't have food, gave money when we went without, and provided support when I felt all alone. We love you very much!

I could not possibly thank all of the people that were there for us in this one section. Whether you were there for a moment, a month, or a lifetime, thank you for the everything you did.

The prayers, hospital visits, cleaning my house, being my personal chauffeurs, feeding my children, helping us pay bills, bringing us meals, buying clothes and Christmas gifts, repairing my home, buying groceries, and just being there for company and soft foods that could go up a straw.

Special thanks to the Lorraine, C.J. Hicks, Midway, Springfield, Motley, Johnson, Cason, Seals, and Williams families. If I missed any names, please "charge it to my head and not my heart." Each and every one of you means the world to me. Thank you for being our support system!

Introduction

I was born into a home filled with domestic violence. The neighborhoods that I grew up in were filled with sexual horrors. These facts meant that I was doomed to a life of depression, risky sexual behaviors, and dysfunctional relationships.

My father was an alcoholic who was physically and verbally abusive to the women in his life. He beat my mother with his fists, broke her collarbone and her heart.

He beat me with his words and called me his "bitch" as casually as someone would say, "Pass the salt and pepper, please." He beat any thoughts of acceptance and love from a man out of me simply by the example he set.

My choices in men and relationships as a teenager and young woman mirrored my parents' marriage. I was in the same abusive relationship over and over and over again.

Despite how I grew up and my failures in love, I truly believed that one day my soul mate, knight-in-shining armor, or one true love (or whatever fantasy we women like to revel in) would come along on his horse and rescue me from my life that was full of pain and loneliness.

I just wanted to have the NORMAL family that I had always dreamed of having when I was a child. I wanted a family like I thought everyone else had.

As an adult, I vowed that I wouldn't have a marriage like my parents. My husband would be perfect. My children would be perfect. My life would be perfect.

What I didn't quite know was children of abuse are doomed to create the same reality as an adult in which they lived as a child. Many times, it is often worse than what they experienced as a child, unless something or someone comes along to teach them something OTHER than the abuse they've learned.

I was born IN a family of violence, my marriage and children were born OF violence, and my ministry and this book were born OF violence, too. This proves that negative situations and events can birth something positive, something restorative, and something powerful. Why? Because God promises us that ALL things (not some things or most things) "work together for the good of those who love God: those who are called according to his purpose." Romans 8:28

This book is for those that have faced death – literally, spiritually, economically, sexually, emotionally, mentally…whatever your case may be. You CAN bounce back from anything, rebuild your life, and allow God to use you to birth something VICTORIOUS out of the violence. Resilience, forgiveness, creativity, love, and wholeness can be born of adversity. It's time to take back your life. I pray this book does this for you!

Love,

Kimya

Prologue: Not My Baby!

Watching her drift in and out of consciousness was more than I could take. I jumped onto the juice-stained, ABC rug and shook her shoeless foot.

"Corinne! Corinne! Wake up! Baby, I love you."

Her eyes flickered opened for a second, and she caught a glimpse of me.

Sheriff Jones demanded, "Don't do that to her. You need to do something productive. That is not helping anyone, especially not her."

In an effort to distract me, he pointed sternly in the direction of the chair. "Get back into that seat and read the sign on the wall."

I stared at that Days of the Week poster. "I don't want to read any damned sign!" I shouted.

I looked at my precious baby lying on the white, cold, tiled floor. Blood poured down her freshly-braided cornrows, and her eyes rolled in the back of her head. She vomited oceans of green bile on her blue Super Girl shirt. These images sent feelings of devastation through me.

Sheriff Jones rubbed her arms and gently called her name. "Corinne...Corinne...sweetie...stay with me..." He tried to keep her awake.

I reluctantly slid back into that yellow toddler chair. I didn't know what to do about her...me...anything.

On top of that, all I felt was pain. I tried holding my head over to my right side. Every beat of my heart sent a gush of blood and pain to the left side of my neck, forming a clot from the bullet jammed there. This made it increasingly hard to straighten my head or speak.

I started breathing erratically.

The hole from the bullet that pierced the side of my face produced a salty river of thick, warm liquid in my mouth that I couldn't swallow or spit out. All I could do is let it run. My mouth no longer worked.

I heaved air in desperation because I couldn't hold the tears back any longer.

The pain...

The memory of what happened just five minutes ago...

My baby...would she live or die?

So many thoughts sped through my mind like an out of control locomotive...

I felt so helpless.

I tried talking to her, but she could no longer respond to me.

Did she know I loved her more than anything?

Did she know she was my sunshine?

Did she know she didn't deserve this?

4

My tears washed all the blood out of my face and onto my white shirt that was already darkened from my other wounds. I was sobbing uncontrollably now.

I began rocking in the chair to try to deal with the excruciating pain, but all I could do was think about her and my son, Theron.

Oh God! He was at home all alone!

What was going to happen to my son?

If that monster could do this to her, what would he do to my son?

Oh my God!

Waves of devastating pain now possessed my body as I shook in complete heartbreak.

All I could do was pray out loud and repeat over and over again: "Holy Spirit...please don't let him take my baby from me. Please don't let him take my baby. Not my baby."

Chapter 1: Santa Claus is Officially Dead!

Ever since I was five, I felt like someone always had their hands or body on top of my body. Touching my vagina. Rubbing me. Humping me. Simulating sex with me. Boys. Girls. Men.

To begin with, there was nothing but boys in my small neighborhood. There was only one other girl named Teresa whose mother rarely let her come out to play, so I had to play with boys...all the time.

This neighborhood was nice. I mean, there were middle income families with their middle-income cars with their middle-income homes and their middle-income children...boys...lots of them.

And because my dad wanted a boy so badly, he treated me like one. So, I built model trains, flew model planes, and played all day in the mud until I was covered with stains. So, when the fifth and sixth grade boys came to pick me up to "play," my parents let me go outside with them.

No big deal.

When the boys formed a secret, boys-only club, complete with a password, I wanted in!

They told me that I had to pass their "initiation" in order to hang out with them.

First test: I had to be able to climb up a ladder to the tallest tree. So, I showed them I could do it.

Second Test: They asked if I knew how to hop over the fence. I exhibited my hopping ability like a champ.

They told me I had one **last test,** and I could play with them. I could be in their club. I could be included. I was so excited that I was willing to do anything. So, at the age of five, I was taken to a mobile storage unit and was told that the only way I could be in their club was to put all of their penises in my mouth. So, at the age of five, I was introduced to the unimaginable.

This opened up the floodgates of the boys in the neighborhood wanting to see if Kim could "come out to play." So, when the boys came to the door to ask if they could take me up the street to play with Teresa, my mother thought nothing of it.

Mommy didn't know that I had to run like someone escaping slavery every day when school was released because if I didn't, "they" would catch me and hump me, grind me, and touch me until their sexual desires were gratified.

They were all sweet, well-mannered, middle-class fifth and sixth grade boys, weren't they? Did the thought ever cross my mother's mind that they would want to sexually assault her five-year-old baby? No, of course not.

One day, she sent me off with D'Angelo and the white boy whose name I do not remember. For the sake of this memory, let's call him Bologna because he always smelled like bologna.

And where did they take me? Off to the woods behind the school across the street from our house. They proceeded to try to penetrate my five-year-old vagina and anus. When they couldn't, they got mad. Really mad! They started tearing down vines, leaves, and trees and shouting. They screamed and growled like rabid animals. They told me that if I ever told anyone, they would destroy me the way they destroyed the forest that day.

And then they left me in the woods with my pants down and my vagina and bottom sore.

Alone to wander for what seemed like hours.

Alone and lost.

Alone and crying.

Circling round and round and round and round until I found God.

Something told me to go a different way, through a path I hadn't considered, and I ended up about three miles from my home in the parking lot of a grocery store, where a white, elderly couple took me home after I asked them, "Are you Christian?"

They answered with a jovial laugh and said, "Yes, we are."

They took me home with scratches all over my face, neck, and back from the brambles, thorns, and branches.

They took me home with remnants of the woods in my hair from where I was laid down and assaulted.

I told my mom I had been playing and got lost from Teresa, and these people brought me home. She didn't ask any questions.

I began to feel like I had a "touch me" sign on my back. I was always told how pretty I was and that always ended in touching. The touching that was disgusting to me at five, and then I started to like it. The body just responds to touch, no matter who is doing the touching.

Then others touching me birthed me touching others as well until there was nothing but all-out child orgies in many homes where I went until all of THEIR "don't you tells" and "I'm going to hurt you if you do" and "you're the one that's going to get in trouble if you do" began to resonate with me and I stopped it. Somewhat.

You can't open up the doors of perversion and not expect evil to walk in. There were many times that I asked, "Why me Lord? I didn't ask for that. Who would look at a five-year-old and get turned on?" Without answers and a way to channel the awakening of my sexual desires well before they should've been aroused, I began searching for love through sex as a teenager.

In my teens, I became hypersexual. I slept with many men before I was even twenty years old. I say men because, at the age of fourteen, I was with the twenty-seven-year-old relative of a neighbor. I had a sleepover at her house. He entered her room one night, pulled me onto the floor, put his hand over my mouth, and told me that it would only take him two minutes to do what he needed to do. "Watch the clock," he said. Maybe I shouldn't have told him that I thought he was cute. I foolishly thought this meant I was good enough to be wanted by a man.

The first boy I really fell in love with would get high on Love Boat[1], and he would put a gun to my head, shove his penis into my mouth, and punch me repeatedly to perform oral sex on him. Maybe I should've just complied with his request the first time he asked, and it wouldn't have led to all of that. At least that's what he said. And then an "I'm sorry."

By the time I was sixteen, my boyfriends were twenty, twenty-one, and twenty-two respectively. I felt worth something because, after all, a "MAN" wanted me, right? All of them wanted nothing but sex. All of them abused me physically, sexually, verbally, and emotionally.

I learned one lesson that was detrimental to my emotional health and view of relationships: I was pretty and all men wanted from me was sex.

That's it. I was worth no more than the pleasure I could provide.

My negative self-image had been birthed from violence. That violence took control of my mind and spirit, and there were times when I wanted to die because I felt worthless. I tried to cut myself, but I didn't have the courage to cut deep enough. I would take pills and pray to God to just take me in my sleep and would be angry when I woke up in the morning.

I started going to Grady Hospital at fifteen and checked myself in the teen program there. They had a clinic where teens could self-refer for counseling and contraception.

---

[1] Marijuana soaked in formaldehyde

I began speaking to a wonderful counselor that kept me from thinking about suicide…for the time being.

By the time I was nineteen, I slowed down considerably. I had fallen in love with an unpredictable man who was estranged from his family and searching for the meaning of his life through [2]bangin' and slangin' dope. Everybody called him "Snow." He was a young man, the same age as me, but he was somewhat taller. He was about 6'2", had perfect, ivory-colored skin, [3]a gold grill, and a large bald eagle tattooed across his back. Me? With a white boy? (My father would've had a fit.)

Snow never held a job more than a couple of weeks to [4]"reup" on his next "50." He had been selling dope since he was nine, but he was someone who promised that he'd never hurt me. He was the "love" I had been looking for. Although, like all the rest of them, we had sex everywhere we could find an opportunity—his uncle's house, my mother's house, his mother's house, the car, his friend's house, hotels, and motels (you get the picture)—he made me feel that I was worth more than the pleasure I could provide. He promised me forever, and I believed him.

---

[2] Term means to sell illegal drugs

[3] means an overlay of gold across the top and/or bottom of someone's teeth

[4] This term means to purchase a certain amount of crack cocaine

---

12

Something transpired between us that I felt would leave me scarred for life. Something ugly and revolting. I can't talk much about that to protect the innocent and the guilty, but let's just say that it forever altered how I viewed the course of my life. Let's just say that I loved a man that loved being with other women. In that relationship, I acquired all the trappings of being in love with a womanizer.

I thought no one else would want me, and I made him promise to never leave me. He didn't keep that promise. He exploited it!

That relationship left me full of trust issues and empty on love...especially self-love. When you feel like you're not good enough, unlovable, fat, undesirable, you feel like less is all you deserve. So, you begin to settle for less. Loving Snow killed Santa Claus.

Santa Claus was my metaphor for the idea of love. I used to go around telling everyone: "I believe in Santa Claus." I was such a hopeless romantic at heart. It really just meant that despite all of my heartache, abuse, rapes, and broken promises, I still believed in true love. If I waited patiently and was a better girlfriend, a better lover, more understanding, cooked better, and cleaned better, my HIM would be faithful and choose to be with me above all the other women in his life; however, nothing changed. In my twisted way of thinking, I wanted him to love me like he loved his other women. I thought my love and devotion could change him. I was wrong. The one lie that women believe is that we can change a man. The one lie that men believe is that we won't leave.

But I did leave.

13

Spotlight on Abuse – Sexual Abuse: Just

know that abuse is never your fault. Rape, molestation, and incest are always about the perpetrator. He is guilty—not you! Sexual abuse can open spiritual doors that many years later will surface as other problems. As a sexual abuse survivor, you may experience:

- **Guilt, shame, and blame.** Don't feel guilty about not being able to stop the abuse or even enjoying the physical pleasure you experienced from the abuse.
- **Depression, low self-esteem, and eating disorders.** You may feel like you are unworthy, dirty, ugly, or fat. These ideas may have been put in your head as a result of the verbal and/or emotional abuse inflicted on you by your abuser. Some of these thoughts may lead you to overeat, binge and purge, or become anorexic. At other times, your depression could lead you to feel so worthless that you become suicidal.
- **Difficulty with Intimacy in relationships.** You may feel like you can't be intimate with someone you really love due to flashbacks and memories. You may even have difficulty establishing trust, live under constant fear of being "different or weird," and have trouble starting new relationships. Finally, you may even find yourself involved with abusive relationship after abusive relationship. ("Adult Survivors," n.d.)

- **Sexual difficulties**. You may experience sexual dysfunction as a result of the abuse. You may lack interest in sex, approach it as your duty or a chore, or experience feelings of disgust or guilt. You may even have difficulty becoming aroused or reaching orgasm. You may develop "nympho syndrome," which causes you to seek out several sexual partners or encounters to be your security blanket or pacifier—substituting sex for love.

What can you do about it?

Matthew 6:12-15 "12 And forgive us our debts, as we also have forgiven our debtors. 13 And do not bring us into temptation, but deliver us from the evil one. For Yours is the kingdom and the power and the glory forever. Amen. [14]For if you forgive people their wrongdoing, your heavenly Father will forgive you as well. [15]But if you don't forgive people, your Father will not forgive your wrongdoing."

In order to live free of the guilt, shame, depression, low self-esteem, and other things you've acquired as a result of the abuse, you must pray and ask your heavenly Father to help you forgive the person who wronged you. You don't have to live with the bitterness and resentment associated with it. If you are having trouble forgiving yourself (even though you've done nothing wrong), seek to forgive yourself as well. Next, you should consider starting therapy with a good counselor or psychologist. You can have your joy restored! Take the first step today!

Pray: Father God, cleanse me of all the shame of the past. Help me to realize there is no condemnation in Christ Jesus. Help me to walk in the freedom you've designated for your children. Help me to have healthy relationships now and in the future. Help me not to characterize other men by what someone else has done to me. Father, help me acknowledge that I am your marvelously crafted handiwork and I deserve Your Best. Help me to receive the joy filled future that you have set for me. In Jesus's name I pray, Amen.

Chapter 2: Desperately Seeking Love

The only positive things from my years of looking for love in all the wrong places were my children. Theron (we call him T.J.), my first treasure, has the most beautiful dark brown, sun-kissed complexion with a smile to melt your heart. He has a football player physique, Major Motion picture ambitions, and a love of fighting certain injustices in the world.

T.J.'s stubborn persistence can come off as arrogant, but he is truly passionate about the things he cares about. Most times his passion to discuss these issues arise at 5 a.m., but I love it!

My other treasure is my daughter, Corinne. She has a perfectly placed dimple right beneath her eye that seems to cause her eye to twinkle whenever she smiles.

Corinne is so generous; she is quick to share everything she has with anyone in need. She is my tough, athletic, and compassionate "little girl" with BIG dreams of playing professional sports for the WNBA and Major League Soccer, as well as operating a five-star restaurant, AND becoming the next award-winning physician.

Why God chose me to birth the beauty of these two glorious souls is a wonder to me. Being their mother has been the hardest and most rewarding privilege ever given to me. I often wondered how two people so beautiful could come from someone who felt so damaged and worthless inside. After looking back at my relationships and the choices I made, I wanted something better for them.

After leaving Snow, I cast myself into a life of celibacy. Me? The self-proclaimed nympho? Yes, me. So, for two and a half years, I waited and abstained, and I attained a valuable piece of information that changed how I viewed the importance of a relationship with a man. Didn't say it was right. Just said that my thoughts changed.

I thought that being married was the answer to all of my problems. I reasoned it didn't work out with the men I had been involved with because they just couldn't be faithful and apparently, I wasn't good enough or I HAD to be doing something to make them so angry to want to keep hurting me.

Therefore, I still felt that a man, another man, would solve my financial problems, my children's need for a father, my need for companionship, my need for sex (did I mention that I took a vow of celibacy?), and all my other problems. So, I turned to God for the answers, somewhat...

During one of the many Bible studies we had on Wednesday afternoons at Midway Elementary School, where I was employed, I discovered through a scripture in Isaiah 54:5 that God was my husband.

Our Bible study coordinator, and my fellow first grade teacher, read to us in her regal Nigerian accent: "Indeed, your husband is your Maker-His name is Yahweh of Hosts-and the Holy One of Israel is your Redeemer; He is called the God of all the earth."

1. I thought, "If God is my husband, then, shoot, I can quit this job right now, stay at home to take care of my children, AND Go back to school to get my master's degree like I always planned to do with an earthly husband."
2. God would take care of all my problems.

Armed with this new information, I devoted myself to taking my relationship with God to a deeper level. Within days of our Bible study, I stepped out on faith and quit my job of ten years to pursue my master's degree and help Theron make a smooth transition from elementary to middle school.

Equipped with a new mindset and ready to take the world by storm, I was the happiest I'd been in years, but there was one thing missing—I still REALLY wanted to be married!

It seemed as though all I ever talked about was being married. My friends at school created a proverbial boat of single women, and I was NOT going to be the last one in it. No, ma'am.

I began to "speak into the atmosphere"that by the end of the next year, I would be married. I sat on my comforter with the red and brown swirls, eating my grapes and honey-roasted peanuts, and turned the volume all the way up on Mary J. Blige's "Be Without You."

I made a list in my diary about what I wanted in a man:

1. Taller than me
2. Handsome
3. Could please me sexually (hey, God knew what I needed)
4. Loved the Lord
5. Good job (no more street dudes)
6. Loved and respected me and my kids
7. Spent time with my kids
8. Never been involved in a homosexual relationship
9. Drug- and alcohol-free.

"Done! That sounds about right." I jumped off the bed and headed for my closet. "Ok, time for task number two."

I stood on one side of my hot closet, working feverishly to clean it out—moving boxes, dresses, shoes, papers, and books to only one side of the closet.

Seeing those books made me think about all of the things I was doing to prepare myself for my new husband. I bought self-help books, listened to the prophets that visited our church, took classes, joined the singles ministry, and went to all the conferences that encouraged us to begin preparing for our husbands that we had been praying for. Never thought that maybe he should be preparing for me.

Oh sure, lots of warnings came from well-meaning church folks and friends. They informed me to be careful because the "imposter always comes before the real thing."

Some close friends felt obligated to tell me that I shouldn't be in a rush to get married because it wouldn't be all that I thought it would be. I convinced myself that they were just jealous because their own marriages were either not going well or had already failed miserably.

Besides that, my hormones were in overdrive, and I knew that due to my celibacy, I couldn't JUST have casual sex. Being molested as a child and subsequently raped as a teenager caused a door of sexual promiscuity to be opened in my life. I had to have sex...a lot. I craved and desired it all the time. I knew that God would not be happy with that decision so I had to get married and hurry along this process.

The sound of running feet coming up the stairs broke the rhythm of Kirk Franklin's "Lookin for You" playing on my CD player...and my thoughts.

My chubby-faced cherub came bounding into my room with her pink and blue Barbie nightgown. She kicked off her slippers, hopped up on my bed, and asked, "Mommy, can I sleep in your bed tonight?"

Looking back at her from the inside of my closet, I smiled and answered, "No, baby."

Now those big, beautiful, brown eyes looked at me intently, and she slowly asked, "Whyyyyyy not?"

I walked over to the bed, sat down beside her, and hugged her close to me. She had just finished her bath and smelled just like baby powder. I loved that! Even though she was five years old, the smell made me feel as if she were still my baby.

"Because my husband is coming, Corinne."

"Well, where is he Mommy?"

"He is on the way, sweetie. I have been praying for him, and God has answered my prayers."

Without saying another word, she shrugged her shoulders, jumped off the bed, slipped her fuzzy pink slippers back on her feet, and headed out of my room.

She stopped, turned around, and announced, "Mommy, I want a daddy like Caillou, okay?"

Not being able to hold back my laughter, I chuckled to myself and imagined Corinne hanging out with my husband that looked and acted like the imaginary PBS dad.

Nah, I thought to myself, but instead said," Ok, Corinne. I will be sure to keep that in mind."

Surprisingly, two weeks later, a guest pastor came to my church and preached about the "24-Hour Miracle." He asked us to sow a $1,000 seed, and in a 24-hour period, something we had been praying for would be answered.

Interestingly enough, Theron and Corinne's dad had just ended a relationship, and we had a discussion about whether or not we should get back together. We had already gone back and forth for years.

I had been praying for a husband. Was HE the husband that I had been praying for?

Was I supposed to get back with him for the umpteenth time?

Was I supposed to wait on someone new?

Well I didn't have $1,000, and I knew that God knew my heart. So, I gave $24 in the offering and got down on my knees right there in between the chairs and asked, "Please, Father. If their Father is not the man I am supposed to be with, make that clear, and please send me the person that I AM supposed to be with."

Well, let's just say this scenario made me realize that God is not a genie in a bottle where we can just rub a magic lamp and he will answer all our prayers simply because we [5]"sowed a seed". It doesn't say that in the Bible anywhere—believe me, I looked.

It wasn't long thereafter that the children's father and I decided that we did not want to give it one more try. He started dating someone else, and I met the man that I THOUGHT was the answer to all my prayers.

And God was about to show me to be careful what I asked for.

---

[5] gave money in an offering at church

Chapter 3: Working on a First Date

Just one month after my experience at church, Miyoshi—my beautiful, highly-fashionable neighbor-turned-friend—sent her brother, Harry, over to my house because my back door had been mysteriously shattered by some person or object. He was tall with caramel colored skin and a short clean-cut fade.

Anyway, I purchased a new door from Home Depot in hopes that Harry could put the new door in for me.

Once upon a time Miyoshi tried to [6]hook us up, but it never panned out too much more than an awesome friendship. Since we'd become such good friends, Harry wanted to introduce me to his old childhood friend named Terrence.

---

[6] attempt to get us to date each other

I had just quit my job at Midway Elementary and started doing things to improve my home and health; therefore, the last thing I was thinking about at the time was starting a relationship with someone that *Harry* was trying to hook me up with. I always joked with him that he had more than enough women so I was not interested in anyone he wanted to introduce to me.

Leaning against the garage door in his yellow polo, blue jeans, and brown flip flops Harry announced, "I'm telling you—Terry is your husband."

"Harry, I don't want to meet any man that is friends with you. You know what they say...birds of a feather flock together," I stated adamantly with my hand on my hip to indicate the seriousness of my statement.

Rolling his eyes as far back in his head as he could and picking under his long fingernails, Harry let out a sigh and said, "Well, if Terry doesn't come to help me, you just won't get your door put in today. I need help, girl."

I reluctantly accepted his terms for replacing my door. So, before I knew it, we were in my powder-blue 2006 Dodge Caravan, going to pick up Terry because, amongst other things, Terry did not have a car. That was a definite no-no!

After parking in the gated apartment community, Harry got out of the van and ran up three flights of steps to Terry's apartment. I was too busy trying to stay cool (pushing the AC to the max point seemed to help). Harry came down and got back into the van almost immediately.

Moments later, Terry walked down the three flights of stairs and across the parking lot toward my vehicle.

Harry began nodding in his direction, nodding in my direction, and hitting my leg at the same time. He said, "Hmm. Hmm. What do you think?"

Just as he got into the van, I mumbled, "I don't think nothing."

"Hello," he said.

"Hi, I'm Kimya."

Harry turned and looked at Terry while interrupting me. "Her name is Kim. Don't nobody call her Kimya." We both started laughing. Well, Kim- yuh (he still didn't say it right), this is my boy Terry from back home that I was telling' you about."

"Nice to meet you, ma'am. My name is Terrence."

Harry threw up his hands and started laughing. "I guess everybody changin' their name."

On the way back to my house, they went on talking about whatever they were talking about. I had my own thoughts. Even though I told Harry I didn't think anything about Terrence when he walked down the steps, I did think he was a little fine. Ok, a LOT fine.

I am not sure if he actually was eye candy or if it was the two and a half years of self- proclaimed celibacy talking to me, but as Ciara's hook to Field Mob's "So What" came through my speakers, his clothing could not hide the obvious muscular physique, but I tried hard to hide what I was thinking.

Terrence was just a bit taller than me. He had ebony colored skin with a bald head. Oh, I absolutely love a man with a bald head! You could tell that he worked out even beneath his blue button-down shirt and when he smiled, he had the brightest, straightest, whitest teeth of anybody I had ever seen. He reminded me of that man in that Janet Jackson video, "Love Will Never Do Without You," from back in the day.

But that was all I could waste my time thinking about because he did not have a car and I was not in the business of going to pick up gentlemen—so I quickly dismissed any short-lived fantasies of seeing what lay beneath that clothing ensemble. Plus, when he got into the car, the strong smell of cigarettes came with him. Yuck!

While working on the door, Terrence informed me that he was much more interested in working than spending time with any woman. Why he told me that, I don't know. I was NOT interested in him either. I was only interested in getting my house painted, so I thought I would ask Terrence to paint it. Apparently, while dropping him off, Harry gave him my number because he called me within days.

I had just sat down to eat the scrambled eggs, sausage, and pancakes that I made for my children and me when the phone rang.

"Hello."

"Hi, this is Terrence. Keith's friend. Did you still want to get your house painted?"

"Wow. Hello. Did Harry give you my number?"

"Harry?"

"Yes, Keith's real name is Harry. But yes, I do. How much will you charge me to paint my entire downstairs and the hallway upstairs?" I asked as I paced around my kitchen, trying to scoop some eggs into my mouth.

"$600," he answered without hesitation.

I almost choked. "Well, I'm sorry, but I simply can't afford that. I am not trying to insult you or anything, but I was not sure of the going rate for such things, so I only set aside $300 for painting."

Taking a deep breath, he agreed to my price and told me that he wanted to start working right away. I agreed to pick him up the next day at 7:00 a.m.

The next day, I picked Terrence up at the Texaco on the corner of Panola and Fairington Road. He was wearing a dark blue polo shirt with his khaki pants. Nothing was special about him that day. In fact, I had no idea that he had any interest in me whatsoever.

We drove around to Lowe's and Home Depot in search of the best paint. We began talking about all kinds of things: hanging sheetrock, country living, and relationships—how men handle things and how women handle things. I told him all about what I wanted in a man and what I *thought* my life would be like when I finally married the man of my dreams.

On the way to my house, Terrence remarked rather casually, "You need to be careful what you tell people. Someone could take that information and use it against you. Stop telling men everything."

I thought that was the most ridiculous thing I had ever heard. In the adult world, it was called being transparent. Ironically, I wasn't even thinking about starting a relationship with him and how we even got on the topic of relationships escapes my memory.

Little did I know he meant every word of what he said in that moment. I gave him the blueprint to my deception.

Within one week, Terrence painted my house beautifully, and when he was almost finished, he called me and asked me out on a date.

It was a rather cute way of asking, if I may say so myself. You see, Terrence was a down-home country boy with what I call an "aw-shucks," Gomer Pyle set of manners. Everything was "yes, ma'am" and "no, ma'am." He had a quiet, gentle spirit that I had not witnessed in any man before.

It was late Saturday afternoon, and I was up finishing up my morning cleaning routine when the phone rang.

"Hello."

"Hello, ma'am. Are you gon' eat?"

I said in a little sing-song voice, "Ummmm, nooooo. I mean, yessss. I mean, what do you mean, Terrence?" I sank down into the soft contours of my brown, leather couch. I had just started cooking spaghetti for my children for dinner and had to sit down to make sure I heard him correctly.

He replied, "Well, I'm gon' eat, and I wanted to know if ya'll wanna come with me?"

I started laughing, "Who is ya'll?"

"You and your chillun'."

"Oh no, I am a big girl, and I can go eat all by myself. They are not going."

I was not in the business of taking my children around people I went out on dates with. They were too vulnerable and fell in love with people quickly. They were a lot like their mom.

"Well, if you come and pick me up," he said, "I'll put gas in your car, and we can go down to Atlantic City."

"You mean...Atlantic Station?" I said as I got off the couch and went back into the kitchen so I could quickly finish cooking dinner.

Atlantic Station is a neighborhood in Midtown Atlanta. It has some amazing shopping and restaurants.

"Yea. I heard a lot of peoples say it was good food down there," he answered.

I was overjoyed to accept his offer because I hadn't had a date in almost three years, and I hadn't ever been to Atlantic Station. So, I agreed to pick him up at four, hung up the phone, threw the garlic bread into the oven quickly, made the tropical punch Kool-Aid, and tossed the salad together so my children could eat.

After I made sure they were fed, I ran upstairs and jumped into the shower. I was excited to use my new Bath and Body Works Sweet Pea shower gel and lotion. I picked out a two-piece black and white halter-style top and mini skirt outfit that was sexy but not too revealing. My hair looked like a hot mess so I pulled it up onto my head, pulled a tight, elastic band around it, and clipped a long ponytail to it.

I jumped in the van, put "Shoulder Lean" by Young Dro on repeat, and sang and shoulder danced in the van all the way to Panola Road.

As I turned into his apartment complex, much to my surprise, he was standing outside the gated area. He was wearing a lime green polo shirt with khaki pants. I didn't think the color suited him much (later when we were married, let's just say that shirt miraculously disappeared), but he walked to the side of my van and asked to drive to our destination.

I got out, hugged him, and inhaled cigarettes. Not cute. But, true to his word, first he stopped and filled my tank up with gas and we departed for the Fox Grill located in the heart of Atlantic Station.

I towered above him with my black high heels but he didn't seem to mind. He held the door for me as we walked into the crowded grill, gave the receptionist his name, and waited quietly for a table. After waiting for about forty-five minutes, we were escorted to our table. I ordered the shrimp scampi linguini, and he ordered the Cobb salad sans the avocado.

I enjoyed talking to him about the triumphs and pitfalls of my past relationships over the sounds of clanging dishes, loud conversations, and televisions blaring in the distance. I told him all the things I didn't like, all the things THEY did wrong, and how I was the victim in a multitude of relationships gone bad. In the beginning, I was nervous, and I could tell he was too. My nervousness usually leads to immense talking so I began by giving him the blueprint of what I wanted in a man, and he began eagerly taking it all in.

He didn't talk much at all. I just thought that he was a good listener and that was great for me since the men in my past typically did not care about what I thought or felt or said. So, for me, this was a welcomed change.

During the course of dinner, Terrence asked me if he could kiss me. I smiled sheepishly, batted my eyelashes, and told him yes. Much to my surprise, he stood up, walked beside me, and gave me a kiss on my cheek. This was definitely different!

Our date ended on a sweet note with him giving me a hug as I dropped him off at his apartment.

"So, I am going to take you out on your birthday," he said.

"Okay," I said, smiling from ear to ear.

I drove home thinking that maybe this man could turn into something very positive in my life. I could even look past the cigarette smell...maybe.

Chapter 4: Looking for Trouble

Two weeks after our first date, he took me out to the Apache Cafe for my birthday.

I bought a brown wrap dress from our local department store that Miyoshi picked out for me. It showed just enough cleavage to get his attention, but not too much so that he would think he was getting any of my goodies[7].

The drive downtown was a memorable one. I have always loved the way the city looked at night with the buildings all lit up like a Christmas tree. It was simply breathtaking.

I rolled down my window and took in the breeze and loudly sang along to "Unpredictable." That Jamie Foxx sure could sing.

In the true style of being a gentleman, he held the door as we walked into the tiny café.

---

[7] sexual activity with a female

He pulled the chair out for me at our table that was covered in white linen. The small, smoky room had finger-snapping, candle-lit ambiance.

We listened to various artists, from singers to poets, that performed pieces on...I do not know. I was too intrigued with this dark, country man, that was nothing like any other man I had ever been with to pay attention to the performances.

The food was awesome, too! I had some jerk wings that were the most delicious I had ever tasted. They were slightly sweet, slightly hot, and cooked to perfection. With those, I had one drink, Sex on the Beach, and couldn't handle it. Ok, I will admit it: I am a lightweight. I am not a heavy drinker, and if someone makes it right, one is all it takes.

After the next few poets, I was ready to go home. I had on some high heels that I definitely could NOT walk in, and Terrence, being the gentleman that he was, went out to my van to retrieve my flip flops. Do you believe that he helped me slip my heels off and my flip flops on?! I thought I was in love! We walked out of the club hand in hand as HIS other hand clutched my prized possessions: my brown, strappy heels.

Oh, my goodness. Had God finally answered my prayers? He surely seemed perfect. Carrying my heels?! Yaaaasssss! This had to be a dream!

My thoughts were interrupted by his asking me if I thought I could drive myself home. Terrence said that he could drop me off at home and take my van to his apartment. Since I wasn't sure if he would run off with my van or not, I asked him to drive me home, he could sleep on the couch, and I would just take him home in the morning. He reluctantly agreed.

When we got back to my house, I flopped on the couch and put my feet up on the ottoman. He sat on the cushion next to me, and we began a conversation that would seem to go on for hours. My dad was living with me at the time, and he and the children were upstairs sleeping.

Watching him talk, I wondered if he was a good kisser. One of my favorite movies is *Hitch*, and just like in the movie, I was one of those women who believed that you could tell everything about a man by the way he kissed. Personally, I didn't believe that he could kiss because he was soooo country. I just knew that I would run circles around him. So, with that drink talking to me, his lips looked more kissable by the minute, and soooo…I asked him to kiss me.

Well actually, I turned, looked at him directly in the face, and said, "When we were at Atlantic Station two weeks ago, you asked me if you could kiss me and then you kissed me on the cheek. Is that *REALLY* what you wanted to do?"

"Yes." He smiled at me and asked calmly, "Is that what YOU wanted to do?"

"No. I wanted a real kiss."

"Do you want me to kiss you now?"

"Yes, you can kiss me if you know what you're doing."
I chuckled at that one a little bit.

Terrence leaned in close to me and put both of his hands on my face. I closed my eyes, tilted my head back, and felt the press of his soft lips on mine. He swept his lips across both of mine very gently at first and then put his tongue into my mouth, taking command of it. His kiss sent surges of electricity throughout my body in tiny little shockwaves of pleasure that had me wondering what ELSE he had to offer. I wasn't expecting that at all.

"Wow! I wasn't expecting that at all," I whispered when he finally let me go.

"I aim to please, ma'am," he replied with that winning, million-dollar smile.

We talked until about 3 a.m., and then I half-heartedly went to bed, leaving him to sleep on my couch. I took a shower, changed into my pajamas, and lay in the bed, wondering where this date would end up. I started toying with the thought that I had a boyfriend.

A man who liked me.

A man with a job who held my hand, kissed me with passion, held my strappy sandals when I couldn't walk in them, and talked to me until the wee hours of the morning because he was really interested in what I had to say.

I prayed to God about this new man in my life. I didn't know how it was going to go, but I surely liked everything about him so far. The car was no longer an issue either. I mean, he was filling my car up with gas, right? Besides that, his kiss was AWESOME! I just knew that if the kiss was that great, well...I wouldn't allow my mind to dwell on such things. I drifted off to sleep with a big smile on my face.

It wasn't long after our first two dates that I found myself in full make out sessions with Terrence at my house. When you play with fire...well, you know the rest.

The first time he came over to my house after our kiss, my children were at school and my dad was no longer living with me. I was wearing a white halter top with no bra and some jean Capri pants with flip flops. We sat on the couch and began talking, and before I knew it, we began kissing.

The flesh is never satisfied so the kissing was getting too much for me to bear. I wanted more and so did he.

I did not want to have sex with him because I knew it was wrong and I promised God and myself that I would not have sex until marriage, but as he began to rub on the top of my shirt, I couldn't help but want more. I lifted my top all the way up so I could feel the warmth of his hands against my breasts. It had been two years since anyone had touched me like that so I exhaled as he continued to kiss me deeply.

With Terrence lying between my legs on the couch with his hands on my bare skin, I began to develop a deeper yearning for him, but I couldn't stand the pressure anymore so I pushed him off me. I wanted it to go further, but I didn't want it to go any further. I thought I was in control of this little game I was playing.

We could touch and tease one another and not get caught up in it, right?

We were adults, right?

The Bible never said anything about touching one another, did it? We weren't touching each other's private parts so it had to be ok, right?

Yet I kept playing a game that was bound to end in trouble.

Our sexual play continued to escalate over the next two months. It began as innocently as kissing and developed into something much more…much more than I was ready for or bargained for.

I went over to his cousin Nikki's house to see him one day. He lived with her when he moved from Glenwood.

Theron and Corinne went over to my sister's house for the weekend, so I knew we would be able to hang out all weekend.

Immediately upon walking in the door, he began kissing me. For some reason, he led me into Nikki's room.

"We can't play around like this in here. It's wrong, Terrence."

He reassured me that Nikki would not be at home for a couple of days, and we weren't going to have *sex* in her room; we would just fool around.

He suggested that we should take our clothes off.

He said he wouldn't do anything to me and that I could trust him. I believed him; however, our flesh was getting out of control.

There was a moment when I thought he was going to penetrate me, and I interrupted, "Terrence, I want to wait until I get married before we have sex. How do you feel about that?

"Okay," he replied. "Why do you want to do that?"

"Well, the Bible teaches us that sex before marriage is wrong, and I don't want to do that anymore. I have always had sex in my other relationships, and this time I want to do things the right way. How do you feel about us just playing around and enjoying one another until we decide to get married?"

"Okay."

"Okay? Just like that, okay?" I asked in a shocked tone.

"Yes. Okay. If that's what you want to do, I will do it," he said.

I put my head on his chest and listened to his heartbeat. In that moment, I felt so safe in his arms.

"Wow, Terrence. You are so perfect. You bring me flowers, and you even share your French fries with me."

"What?" We both started laughing.

"Yep. You have tea parties with my daughter, play basketball with my son, and now you are saying you are willing to wait to have sex with me until we're married."

I started crying soft tears onto his chest. "I just never had..."

"Kim, look at me, baby."

I tried to wipe the tears from my eyes as I looked up at him.

"I love you. I will do whatever it takes to make you happy. I love them kids, too. I ain't like them other boys you messed around with. I am a man. A man takes care of his woman. He takes care of his family. I watched my dad take care of my ma. He loves that woman, and he shows her every day. I promise to do that for you too if you give me a chance."

I put my head back on his chest and started listening to his heartbeat again.

"You are so perfect, Terrence."

"Now, I ain't perfect."

"Yes, you are. Perfect for me...."

We decided that staying in that bed was too tempting and decided to take a drive to downtown Atlanta to the Varsity to get some hotdogs and fries. Of course, just one order of fries for him, so he could share with me.

And I felt like I was in heaven that night and all the way home.

That promise to stay celibate didn't last. It was only a matter of time.

Within a week of going to see him at his cousin's, it happened.

Sex with Terrence was explosive!

He was such a good lover that I believe sex was one of the major factors that got me to put my defenses down and ignore all the things in him that I said I didn't want in a man:

1. Messed up finances
2. No car

3. No children
4. Would not go to church with me.

Sex covers a multitude of sins. The Bible says that "love covers a multitude of sins," but when you are quick to share your body with someone, the soul ties that are formed will prevent you from seeing the true man that lies behind the mask.

Prior to being with him, I hadn't experienced what an orgasm was supposed to feel like. This is the reason that God warns us not to have sex outside of marriage. Sex formed a bond with Terrence that would not be easily broken. This was not love. It was lust—pure and simple.

I will never forget that moment when "it" happened. My children had gone to my sister's house, and he spent the night at my house. Terrence began laughing at me and asking me if I were okay—probably because I began coughing and my body was shaking uncontrollably.

He jumped up out of bed, clapped his hands, and pumped his fist in the air in a sign of victory. He said, "Yes, I got her!"

Since sex was a game of winning and losing in my mind, I simply wrote this off as a winning moment for him. Looking back on it, I now realize he meant something deeper. Much deeper.

Sex was so good with Terrence that I broke another standard of mine, and he started living with us. Living with Terrence put my relationship with God in jeopardy. I let him come between my value system and my love for God. The soul tie was created.

On October 20, 2006, I wrote in my journal:

Father,Good morning.

I have been talking to Kelly and Gretchen, as You know, about sexual sins. As You know, I've been celibate for two and a half years; however, in the last two weeks, I have had sex with Terrence about six or seven times. Jehovah, forgive me.

I love this man deeply. In my heart of hearts, I feel he loves me too. But I don't love him more than I love You. And I know he doesn't love me more than You do. You have brought me through so much—You, Jesus, and the Holy Spirit. I don't want to grieve you all in that way. It is my heart's desire to remain pure until marriage. His level of spirituality is not exactly where mine is, but Jehovah, I know that all things are possible with You. Please give us the strength and courage to wait until we are married. Let our love for You be stronger than the lust between us.

Father I am asking You in Jesus's name for great and unexpected miracles in our lives because of it. I am going to record Terrence's and my blessings as a result of saying "no" to sex before marriage. Lord, please allow this.
Let Terrence see how serving You is of great benefit to him. Elevate his level of spirituality. Increase and bless the work of his hands as a result. Bring people and resources (money) into his hands. Bring the truck he needs into his hands. Make him prosperous from the crown of his head to the soles of his feet.

I will pray with him this morning. Manifest this in our lives, beginning today. As for me, make our love grow stronger every day. Please let us keep You first in our lives. Let our commitment to one another grow stronger. Let us grow in wisdom, knowledge, and understanding of each other. Please give us the blessing of compromise and seeing the other's point of view.

Please expedite this wedding. Bring and give us the resources (money) to make it happen expeditiously. I will record Your blessings as a testimony to all in this book and proclaim Your goodness all the days of my life. And I will dwell in the house of the Lord forever. Amen!

Love,

Kimya

P.S. You said through Your servant that every time we fornicate, we miss a blessing. So, every time we have an opportunity to fornicate and want to fornicate but don't fornicate, we will receive a blessing. Amen!

I recorded only three miracles between the two of us after I wrote that diary entry. There were only two recorded entries of us not having sex.

Chapter 5: Anger Ignored

Within a month of moving in together, Terrence gave me a slight glimpse of his anger when he was suffering from a migraine headache. Many times, men will begin to take off the mask once you've made a commitment to them. Terrence gave me a fast glimpse of the real him.

One afternoon, he came home early from a construction job because he had a very bad headache. He went upstairs and lay across the bed. Being the nurturing girlfriend that I was, I went upstairs, walked into our bedroom, and asked him if he wanted anything.

He muttered "no" under his breath.

I saw that he was indeed suffering so I sat down on the bed, rubbed his back, and asked him if he wanted any Tylenol or Ibuprofen.

He snapped, "No! Just leave me the hell alone."

Taken aback, I got up from the bed, walked quietly to the door, shut it behind me, and began to cry.

I went down the steps, disillusioned and wondering what happened. My children would be home from school soon so I sucked up the tears and began frying chicken for dinner.

Terrence emerged from the room hours later and came downstairs humming a song, as if nothing happened.

I was sitting at the kitchen table, helping Corinne finish up her homework, when he came downstairs, gave her a hug, walked over to me, kissed the side of my neck, and asked, "What's up?"

I ignored his attempts to speak to me. Corinne began to give him a play-by-play about all her adventures in school that day.

Once he noticed I was quiet, he began questioning me as to what was wrong with me, and I told him to come upstairs with me to our bedroom so we could talk in private about what transpired earlier.

Once upstairs, I told him how I really felt. "Terrence, I don't like it when you yell at me like that. You really hurt my feelings."

"I'm sorry baby," he said and started walking towards me with his arms out to hug me.

He wrapped me up in his arms and held me close with my forehead just near his lips.

"It won't happen again. I just have bad headaches, and I don't like to talk. I just want to be alone in the dark. Don't nothin' help it but time."

He started kissing me on my forehead and walked me to the bed.

"You know I love you baby."

"Yes, I know. I love you, too. I just wanted you to feel better so I..."

He leaned in to kiss my lips and made it up to me...with sex.

I should have paid more attention to the signs in the beginning, but the problem was that Terrence only showed his angry side to my son, Theron, when he was misbehaving. That is one of my greatest regrets because in my heart I never felt right about how he was disciplining my son.

By the time Theron was in the sixth grade his behavior was unbearable. His teachers would call two to four times per week to have me pick him up from school for misbehavior due to his crises that were caused by Asperger's[8].

Theron's behavior intensified so much that in the beginning of that year, I sent him to live with his father. He only came to visit me every other weekend so Terrence did not see him in action; consequently, all of their interactions in that period of time were great!

Terrence would spend time with Theron and his friends on Saturday afternoons. They would shoot hoops in the yard, go to the local putt-putt amusement park, ride go-karts, or talk about how to become a man. I wasn't privy to these conversations, but they made me so happy because my man took such an interest in my son.

Within five months of Theron living with his dad, his father sent him back to live with me. It did not take long for Theron's true colors to shine through, and Terrence got an eye and ear full of Theron's behavior.

---

[8] a form of high functioning Autism where people are characterized with average to high intelligence; however, they may have poor social skills and/or coping strategies in response to stressors

While sitting on the edge of my bed one night, I tried to explain to Terrence, through a stream of tears, that I found it very difficult to get Theron to be obedient, and his coping skills kept him from dealing with anything he deemed to be stressful in a healthy way. I tried to explain that he wasn't a "bad" child and that his actions were a manifestation of his disability.

"Oh," Terrence said. He let out a deep sigh and rolled his eyes. "There ain't nothin' wrong with that boy. You let them white folks put a label on him, and the only thing wrong with him is he been raised by women. I ain't doing nothin' to that boy that wasn't done to me, and I turned out just fine."

I wiped my tears on the back of my hand and began to contemplate what Terrence just told me. I shook my head no.

"But he has been having trouble since he was two years old. He was diagnosed with ADHD in kindergarten and Asperger's syndrome in first grade. He is brilliant and could probably tell you all the classifications of dinosaurs, every movie Disney has made since its inception, and how to invest your money in the stock market, but he cannot handle stress. He will go into 'crisis mode,' which looks like misbehavior, but it really isn't."

Terrence only shook his head and stood up to walk out of the room.

"Another problem with that boy is no one put the fear of God in him. I ain't neva seen nobody act like Theron."

Every child needs to fear one of his parents. I'm still scared of my daddy to this day. I did not play with that man. And boy, if you think he was mean. Ooo weee...you don't want to see my ma when she get mad. That lady is mean as hell. Me and my sister do not mess with them.

People didn't understand the anguish and sense of hopelessness I felt because I did not know how to parent this child. To top it off, relatives, teachers, and strangers felt his behavior was a result of bad parenting. I was caught in the middle of all of this, and I didn't know what in the hell I was doing.

Many nights I cried and asked God to help me with him. People had been telling me that it was my parenting that caused Theron to act out, but I did not feel as though fighting my child was what he needed. Sure, I spanked Theron and Corinne both when they were disobedient and would even curse at them at times (God was still working on me with that one), but I could not see myself fighting with Theron. As a result, well-meaning family members and friends would call me "weak."

So, when Terrence and Theron began to have major fights about things, I questioned my own beliefs and allowed certain things to go on when I should have stopped it. This is one of the things I am most ashamed of.

I was desperate to make this wedding happen, believing wholeheartedly that being married to Terrence would make everything all better with God and my children. I would not be having sex outside of marriage, my children would have a full-time father, and I would be married to the man who truly loved me. So, I ignored the incidents of anger towards me and "discipline" toward my son and decided without a proposal, ring, or any other formality to go ahead and get married. One thing I learned from this choice is that whatever is wrong prior to a marriage, it will only magnify once you say, "I do.

Chapter 6: Here Comes the Bride

I spent the whole weekend before the wedding with my best friends: Kelly, Andria, Tosha, and Rayna. I was so happy! We spent the whole weekend parading around town wearing our tiaras. They wore their pink "BRIDESMAID" shirts, and I wore my white shirt with "B-R-I-D-E" emblazoned in gold across the front.

We waved to everyone like we were in a beauty pageant. That was Andria's idea. She was the grand diva of the group. Andria commanded attention wherever we went with long, black hair gracing the area above her butt—just purchased from her favorite weave store—and cleavage that was purposely placed in a low-cut V-neck shirt. In Sephora, she dictated to the makeup artist what colors would look best on me and acted like she was modest when Kelly asked her to do my makeup for the wedding the next day. She knew she could [9]slay that makeup.

---

[9] apply makeup in a professional way

We dined at our local Applebee's at Stone Crest Mall, drank all kinds of tropical concoctions, laughed, and dreamed about our tomorrows.

We visited my favorite nail spot, On the Edge Nails, where I fought becoming a bridezilla when Andria and I argued (and I won!) about whether she would wear the pink French manicure or her usual all black nails or French white tips.

That night, we had an old-fashioned sleepover in a suite at one of my favorite hotels, courtesy of the mother of one of my son's former football teammates. It was just like I always dreamed it would be. We laughed, joked, cried, and reminisced into the wee morning hours.

Terrence called me to let me know that he had purchased the rings and to tell me about his outing with Harry and Sam—his groomsman and best man.

"Hello, Future Husband."

My friends were making gag faces at me and laughing in the corner. I waved for them to hush while trying not to laugh myself.

"Heyyyy, baby."

"So, what's up, Terrence? Y'all on your way to the strip club?"

"Nah. They wanna go, but I am not into that stuff. They just gon' try to get me drunk."

"Oh, and that's better," I said in a sarcastic tone, and we both started laughing.

"I love you, Kim. Are you ready to be a Roberson?"

"Yes! Of course, I am."

"You know they don't let just anyone be a Roberson. You got to be pretty special."

"Yeah, uh–huh, Terrence. You got to be pretty special that I am going to LET you marry me. You are one lucky man."

He just laughed, and after we said our "good nights" and "I love yous," I happily went right back to the festivities with my girls.

At two a.m., we finally decided to call it a night because I had to get up at five a.m. After all, I had a six o'clock appointment at the hair dresser. "Good night, Miss Motley," Andria said.

"Yes, tomorrow you will no longer be Miss Motley. You will be Mrs. Roberson," Rayna quickly chimed in. I turned and looked at Rayna as I blushed and beamed with pride at the prospect of that. Rayna was my "no nonsense" type of friend. She was beautifully bronzed with skin that would rival any of those girls in the commercials. She had such a caring heart and yet didn't take any mess from anybody around her. She and Tosha sat up and finished making the wedding program CDs for tomorrow. That was one of her gifts to me.

I am so blessed to have friends like them.

The day of my wedding was absolutely beautiful. Even though it was still dark outside, it just FELT beautiful. Kelly woke me up at 5:00 a.m. on Sunday, September 16, 2007 to go to see Vance to get our hair done for one of the happiest days of my life.

Kelly looked a lot like me, or at least that was what people said. She had long, "flowy" hair with golden highlights like Farrah Fawcett. She loved the Lord, but she had a fire in her that would put you in the mind of every character Taraji P. Henson portrayed. Yet she could pray heaven down to Earth at a moment's notice.

I felt a little stressed, which was supposed to be normal; however, no amount of stress could overshadow the pure joy I felt. I jumped in the shower. Afterwards, I pulled on my white, bride's jogging suit I purchased from Victoria's Secret in the mall and bounced out the door.

The week prior, I went to see Vance to get a hair weave. I was a bit nervous about it at first. I'd always wanted a weave, but I didn't know how it was going to turn out. But let me tell you, Vance did an awesome job! I looked GOOD, and you couldn't tell me I wasn't hot!

I emerged from the salon as a vision of absolute beauty (if I may say so myself). Vance turned my straight mane into a cascade of curls that fell just below my shoulders and framed my face. When he turned me around in the chair to face the mirror, I put both of my hands on my cheeks in disbelief and began to cry.

"Oh my God, Vance. This is so pretty. Thank you so much."

Kelly remarked how beautiful I was too, and we both had a "moment" in the salon (we are nothing but a bunch of old sentimental softies that cry in awe at absolutely EVERYTHING).

I couldn't believe the day of my dreams was finally here. I would no longer be alone.

My life was now going to be complete.

My family would be complete.

The perfection I always dreamed of would be made manifest today. I would be married forever to the man that would love me and my children unconditionally.

Or so I thought.

The car ride down the tree-lined streets through the Hollybrook subdivision seemed to take forever. I was so ready to marry this man.

When we arrived at the clubhouse (a little late—it wouldn't be me if I weren't a little late), many of the out-of-town guests had already arrived. Upon stepping out of Kelly's car, the first person to greet me was Terrence's dad, Bo. He immediately came up to me and gave me a big hug. He was a dark, short, stocky man with a kind smile.

His mother came around the car and hugged me also. Mrs. Roberson was a fair-skinned, plump beauty. She was dressed in a golden "mother of the groom" dress. She always reminded me of my aunts in the country. She was always happy, smiling, and, boy, could she cook!

They both told me how beautiful I looked, and they smiled at me so happily. They seemed to be excited about the day as well. We walked into the clubhouse together.

It was a little hot inside the venue and for the life of me, I could not remember how to turn the AC on. I flicked and fussed with the thermostat and was told by my wedding coordinator not to worry about it because she would handle everything. The place was absolutely stunning, which was a wonderful surprise. My friends had to decorate the venue at the last-minute due to some unfortunate circumstances that had arisen with the decorator just a few hours before my ceremony.

White linens, with the modest decorations I spent the last month making on my own, adorned every table. The wedding coordinator illuminated the entire room with small trees wrapped in tiny, white Christmas tree lights. There were tall, paneled candle holders on each corner of the fireplace, which was the area where my nuptials would take place.

Nicole Powell and Deanna Wheeler, my former coworkers, draped the room in cascades of brown and pink tulle that matched my wedding party's attire. There were the CD programs that Rayna created just for us on every table. It was pink and brown with our engagement photo on the front. We even had the nerve to call the CD "The Perfect Love."

I immediately went into the bathroom to begin changing my clothes and trying very hard not to cry, but a few tears managed to escape because I was so happy. I looked at that champagne-colored, strapless dress that Kelly picked out for me and couldn't believe my dreams had come true.

Once all of my girls helped me get bustled, snapped, zipped, and dressed, Tosha smiled at me and began crying.

"You look so beautiful!"

She looked beautiful as well. Her chocolate dress enhanced her warm, tawny complexion. Although it was a little long, she made it look regal.

For a just a moment, I reflected on all she'd done for me throughout the years. She shared food in college (because we were two, almost broke, single parents), allowed me to borrow her car to take my son to multiple hospital visits, and gave me money to make my wedding day dreams come true. With her standing by my side as my bridesmaid, I felt even more emotional.

"Don't do that to me, Tosha. I don't want to start crying, too."

She, Kelly, Andria, and Rayna all hugged me, fighting back tears.

Andria placed the golden tiara with Swarovski crystals on my head, and Kelly and Rayna fussed over the positioning of the veil.

We then got a knock on the door from Susanne Safar, one of my coworkers-turned-friends from my previous school.

"You have a visitor." She beamed.

I received one of my first surprises of the day. The door to the bathroom swung open, and, much to my surprise, my grandfather stood in front of me.

"Big Daddy! You made it!"

I ran to my grandfather and hugged him tightly. He always smelled like freshly starched clothes and chewing tobacco. I loved that smell. My girls left the bathroom to begin lining up for the wedding march.

"Gal, didn't I tell you I's coming."

"Yes, but everyone else told me that you wouldn't be able to make it because you were sick."

"Can't listen to what everybody be tellin' you, gal."

"Okay."

"You got your nerves?" he asked. I knew that meant: "Are you nervous?"

"Yes, sir."

Big Daddy got a very serious look on his face and pointed at me.

"Well, just remember that whatever you got, [10]'vide with him, and whatever he got, he 'vide with you. Or else you ain't neva gon have nothin'. You understand, gal?"

"Yes, sir."

"Okay den. Let's go."

I kissed him on his face as someone snapped pictures of us.

My grandfather grabbed my hand, walked out the bathroom, and literally dragged me down the aisle because I simply could not (and still cannot) walk in heels. At the age of ninety-two, the only man to have loved me and never hurt me walked me down the aisle to marry the man of my dreams.

When my eyes met Terrence's, we both began crying. He looked so proud to be with me in that moment. I walked past members of the Williams, Roberson, and Johnson families—clapping, smiling, and crying all at the same time.

When the officiant asked, "Who gives this woman to be married to this man?"

Big Daddy interrupted, "Wait a minute." He turned toward Terrence.

"You promise you gon' treat her right?"

"Yes, sir," Terrence answered with a smile.

---

[10] My grandfather was telling me to share everything with my husband and he should share everything with me.

"Okay, den. I do," my grandfather said and was escorted to his seat by Andria.

I felt so protected and proud when my granddaddy asked him that.

My grandfather would die a year later and Terrence's answer to that question would upset me the most when I reminded Terrence EVERY TIME he hurt me of his promise he made to my Big Daddy.

At the end of the ceremony, Terrence grabbed me with both hands and dipped me towards the floor as he planted one of the most sensuous and loving kisses on me.

I smiled from ear to ear and couldn't have been happier. I was on such a cloud that when he spoke to Kelly about the nature of my relationship with her, I didn't realize the seriousness of what he said...

"She is mine now. She been bought and paid for."

Kelly and I laughed loudly. "Terrence," I said. "Oh, okay. Now what is that supposed to mean?"

"Yes. She was my friend first. So, you are going to have to share," said Kelly as she continued laughing.

He started laughing too and said, "That means that all that hanging out and talkin' ya'll do is about to be put to an end. It's gonna stop."

We went right on laughing at the silliness of his statement, but only two of us were laughing, and one person was VERY serious.

Spotlight on Abuse - Early Signs: Right

now you may feel like you're floating on cloud, but if you see any of these characteristics in your honey, it COULD signal danger. Some of the characteristics in isolation may not mean anything, but it could be a huge red flag of something much deeper. If he displays a number of the following qualities, it may be time to pump the brakes on this relationship.

- **Isolation**: They may try to cut you off from social supports and find fault with the people who act as your support network. They may say things like: "I want us to spend all of our time together," or "I don't like it when you hang with her because she is trouble." (Grovert, 2008) He may refuse to let you visit friends or family without him ("Red Flags," n.d.)
- **Objectification**: Often sees you as property or a sexual object
- **Social Media Screening:** May screen your calls and demand to know passwords to your social media accounts
- **Rush to Commitment:** Try to push you into a commitment early such as moving in together, making major purchases together, talking about being married and/or having a baby("Red Flags," n.d.)
- **Sweep You Off Your Feet Syndrome:** Seem perfect or "too good to be true," make major purchases for your early in the relationship

(diamonds, trips, purses, shopping trips), and/or giving you large sums of money

- **No Respect for Boundaries:** Break and push your boundaries (pressure you into having sex, "pops up" at places unexpectedly, doesn't' take no for an answer, etc.).
- **Jealousy**: Can be extremely jealous and often accuses you of being with/looking at someone else
- **Bad Mouth Exes:** Talks about his exes in mean, derogatory ways; plays the victim and won't take responsibility for his part in the relationship going wrong (say things like: "My ex was crazy," or "My ex was always the one cheating on me").
- **Anger Outbursts**: Rage out of control for unexplained reasons with you but no one else.

What can you do about it?

Proverbs 14:12 There is a way that seems right to a man, But its end is the way of death.

If you are unsure about your new relationship, begin to pray about it with your Heavenly Father. Place your significant other in social situations where your family members and friends are present. They can often spot when something is wrong, even when you can't. If you are still unsure, speak to a neutral party, such as a domestic violence advocate. She can help you decipher the signs, signals, and language of abuse.

Pray: Father God, in the name of Jesus, open my eyes to see the heart of _____ (fill in the blank)..
Help me to see his true intentions towards me. Father God, help me not to be deceived. Give me peace as I wait on the one you've chosen for me. Fill up the empty places in me.

Wherever I lack self esteem and strength, help me to be stronger. Help me not to settle. Give me eyes that see corruption. Help me to expect and receive your best for me. In Jesus's name, Amen.

Chapter 7: The First Year of Marriage

I never dreamed when I got married that I would be doing worse financially than I did when I was single. IN November, just two months of getting married, we were broke. Terrence took over the finances immediately and decided to start his own business. I thought financial issues were the "norm" with people starting new businesses; however, it was his wasteful spending and unethical business practices that left our finances in a state of emergency.

I decided to buy a thankful journal. If I focused more on what was right in my life versus what was wrong, my spirit may begin to take a different perspective. It was so beautiful...so girly. It was mint green with pink paisley flowers all over it. It seemed like just the right thing to write nothing but God's wonderfulness in it. My hope was that it remained a thankful journal.

One day, our whole state was in a drought crisis, but it had been raining all day! Blankets upon blankets of water showered down on the glass, mimicking the downpour of sadness I felt deep inside.

I guess I should have been happy because Charles, our loan officer at the car dealership, just called me and told me that we should come in to sign the papers for the car loan. Earlier that day, we discovered we had financial issues and were told we wouldn't be able to qualify for the truck. I began to think negatively when that happened, but as usual, God answered my prayers and allowed my husband to have his truck.

By December, just three months after our wedding, we really didn't know how we were going to pay our bills, and we NEEDED everything! Our financial situation went from bad to worse. We needed money for groceries, mortgage, bill for the car, utilities, and Terrence's bills. If it weren't for my cousin, Shadonna and friend Lynn buying groceries for us; my sister, Sandy, charging Christmas gifts for the children on her credit card; and my friend, Gretchen, loaning me money to pay for Terrence's gift, we wouldn't have had much of a Christmas at all.

We seemed to be doing fine, and then as soon as we got married, Terrence slowly stopped giving me the amount of money he was giving me in the beginning. We were in dire straits.

Christmas always made me feel so much better. We just got paid so I went into Michaels and bought some ribbon and other stuff for the house for Christmas.

I wanted to change the colors on tree as well. Miyoshi went with me to pick out the colors for the tree. I was in love with the way she decorated her home year after year, so I knew she would be the perfect one to help me with this little project. We decided on earth tones—green, gold, and copper—for the tree. It would go along perfectly with the colors I had chosen when I decided to let Terrence paint the house over a year ago.

Despite our money troubles, I tried to forget about them by going all out with the decorations for our home. That probably was not the smartest thing to do with the money at the time, but it made me feel better.

I asked Terrence to put up the Christmas lights. He tried to put up a protest it, but I knew just what to do to get my way with him. Sex always worked with him. While he was sitting on the couch, I straddled his lap and kissed him all over his face.

"Terrence, would you please hang up some Christmas lights outside?"

Baby, I am tired. I been workin' all day."

"Wellll, if you are a good little husband and hang up those lights, when you come back in, meet me upstairs, and I will have a little surprise for you."

"I will do it...with yo' spoiled ass."

I started laughing.

It never took much. He gave me one last kiss, and I got up so he could call Harry. He borrowed his tall ladder and went to work on the lights. He looked so sexy up on that ladder in his khaki pants and blue, button-down, collared shirt.

I had always wanted lights on the house. I was always the one person in the neighborhood that didn't have them, and that year I had the most beautiful house display ever. I was so thankful. I had a great family, loving husband, and two of the most wonderful children a woman could ever ask for.

Christmas that year ended up being great. We gave Theron a movie camera so he could begin filming for his budding film career. Corinne received a new Phillips 19" color television. That was all I was able to give them, but they always said, "This is the best Christmas Ever!"

Theron and Corinne's dad picked them up and spent Christmas day with them, so Terrence and I had some much-needed alone time together. We spent Christmas evening having dinner at an all-you-can-eat Chinese food restaurant and making love for the rest of the night. I was in heaven.

Two days after Christmas, I burned my hand badly. The children wanted to help me prepare some dinner for the family. I was frying some chicken, and the oil splattered all over my right hand and thumb. It was so painful.

My wonderful family pitched in to help me for the day. Theron helped me with the laundry and cleaned the kitchen. Corinne swept the floor and helped me finish cooking. On top of that, Terrence came home early, deposited money in the bank for our light bill, took Theron's broken camera back to the store (yes, he broke that brand-new camera), and, of course, tended to my burned hand when he returned. Everything seemed to be going well.

The new year came with so many blessings. My neighbor across the street had been right. When we got married and did things God's way, He WOULD bless our marriage.

I wrote this in my diary on January 2, 2008:

"Happy New Year! Thank you for the wonderful sex I had with my husband last night, the dinner yesterday, money for groceries, Corinne's shoes, and gas for my husband's truck."

Even though I had been worried for so long about our household bills, God sent answers to all our prayers.

To top it all off, my husband was being so romantic. He knew I loved flowers and brought them home for me one night. Terrence picked me up, spun me around, and kissed me all over my face and neck. He started licking me on the face, which I hated and loved at the same time because I knew where it would lead. He told me that he had a surprise for me.

He told me that I could go and take a bath and relax because although he had just gotten off work, he was going to iron the clothes for the week for Corinne and me. He was such the picture-perfect husband during this time. Who knew it would all change?

By June, all hell had broken loose again. We started out at the beginning of the year with a plan AND the money to ensure all of our bills were going to be paid. I had just gotten my refund check from my student loans from college. Terrence wanted to quit working at the hardware store, start his own business, and my support to do so. In January, he asked me to give him all my financial aid and retirement money.

"Kim, I need you to trust me. I am the man of this house. You gotta trust your husband."

"How are we going to pay bills?"

"I am going to pay the bills. You are supposed to submit to what I ask you to do. My dad tells my ma what he gon' do, and she does it. She don't do all this back talk."

Even though I didn't BELIEVE that or want to do that, I wanted to support my husband. I wanted to allow him the opportunity to be responsible. It was the wrong move to make.

We didn't have enough money to pay our mortgage for two months. By June, my mini-van had been repossessed. Terrence said he wanted us to hide it because if we didn't, we would need $1,300 to get it back. Where were we going to get that kind of money?

He demanded that I hide the van when he went to work that day. But I just couldn't do it.

I knew he would be mad at me, but I called the company, pulled into the Wal-Mart parking lot, and called my friend Nichelle to come and pick me up. Nichelle was my sassy dressing, sometimes argumentative friend (though I never saw that side—she just told me she was), who REALLY had a big heart. She could work an incredible mortgage deal by day and bake an impeccable cake by night.

By the time he came home, he was livid. "Why in the hell did you do that?!" he shouted.

"I cannot lie, Terrence. It is wrong. They wanted their van back. I don't want to go to jail"

"Your stupid ass ain't going to no jail! I told you not to do that. I told you to trust your husband."

"Well, I got scared, and you shouldn't ask me to break the law."

"You supposed to respect me."

He got so angry that he walked out of the house and did not come home that night. I was so upset that I called Tosha.

" Girl," I cried to her. "This reminds of what my ex did to me. I know he is with some woman. What should I do? I don't want to lose my husband too."

She gave me some ideas on what I needed to say and do.

No matter how much I tried to do some self-talk to alleviate my fears, I didn't have any peace about where he was or what he was doing. So many thoughts were going through my head...

What if he left me?

Maybe I should've hidden the truck.

I couldn't break the law though. I just couldn't.

I didn't want to go to jail.

When he returned the following morning, he was dressed in the same clothes that he left in the night before.

I hadn't been to sleep all night. He apologized to me, and I apologized to him. We didn't talk about the van anymore.

At times, I felt like my life had been destroyed. In addition to my car being repossessed, Terrence's truck was four months behind. By this time, our cable, gas, internet, and my cell phone had all been disconnected. Terrence had even developed bleeding ulcers due to the stress. My bank accounts were frozen.

Terrence's misuse of finances infiltrated my life and took us on a downward spiral; however, I knew that God promised to provide ALL our need according to His riches in glory through Christ Jesus. I was hoping that because I was going to work next month, things would be better.

Trying to focus on the positive, I thanked God that Terrence was able to pay the electricity bill. Tosha paid the phone bill, and my children's sister's mother, Lynn, and Shadonna helped us with groceries. My neighbor even let us use her pool passes. I could walk my children to the pool daily so they could enjoy their summer. I was determined to find the silver lining in these gray clouds.

As the month went on, slowly but surely, Terrence got money for the water bill. Nichelle gave us her key to her home so we could go over to her house daily to take hot baths and showers. Nichelle was so awesome to us!

By this time, remaining positive seemed impossible and I was growing increasingly depressed and didn't feel like I had strength to do much of anything.

After a while, there was really good news, too! Our gas was turned back on. Andria, turned on the gas in her name for us, and Terrence was able to pay his bill for the truck for one month. Once he made the first payment, the company was willing to work with us; they lowered his payments from $516 to $343. But everything had to go in my name only.

We even had enough money for a date! Terrence took me to Jim and Nick's for dinner. We had the best barbecue ever. My children were at Sandy's for the weekend. I started a new exercise program, and my classroom for my new job at C.J. Hicks was almost complete, and Theron had not had any major temper flare-ups that week.

The biggest surprise of all was getting a new car! I thought that because I had a repossession, I would not be able to get one, but my sister put the car in her name. I could not believe it! I bought a gray 2006 Toyota Camry, paying $365 a month with 10% interest. God was so good!

Things were getting better...or so I thought

Spotlight on Abuse-Economic Abuse:

Economic abuse is one of the most powerful weapons he can use to keep you trapped in the relationship. It crosses all educational, racial, ethnic, religious, economic, and socio-economic lines. Research shows that economic abuse is present in 98% of all abusive relationships. Sometimes it appears once you start a commitment, and other times it starts once you try to leave or have left the relationship.

It is often asked why do people STAY in abusive relationships. One of the top answers given by women is the fear of not being able to care for themselves or their children without the financial help from her significant other. ("About Financial Abuse," n.d.)

Do you feel like your partner is always trying to take your money or control how you spend it? Does he try to keep you from going to school or work? He is doing this not because "it is for your own good," but because he is trying to control you. Economic abuse can look like:

- Forcing YOU to obtain loans and/or applying for loans and credit cards or opening accounts without your consent
- Using your ATM or credit cards without your knowledge
- Giving you an allowance from your own money
- Harassing you at work
- Demanding you turn your paycheck over to him
- Insisting the lease or deed be in his name solely ("Facts about DV and Economic Abuse," 2015)
- Telling you what you can buy with your money

What can you do about it?

1 Timothy 5:8 But if anyone does not provide for his own, that is in his own household, he has denied the faith and is worse than an unbeliever.

Your partner should be providing FOR the household, not taking FROM the household. Seek help through a domestic violence shelter or advocacy agency. Next, obtain a copy of your credit report from all three reporting agencies to assess the damage. Calculate what it would take to live on your own and try to stash away money in a safe place, such as with a trusted friend or in a relative's home. You'll want to keep all of your important documents, car keys, medications, and extra money in a safe place and CREATE a safety plan. A safety plan is a personalized plan that helps you decide on the best course of action to take when a person wants to leave the relationship or within two years of leaving the relationship.

Pray: Father God, I thank you that you did not create me to be abused by someone. I am your child – daughter of the most High. Father, give me a vision of who I am in you. Help me to see the value that you have placed on me. You have given me the ability to create wealth. Give me creative ideas on how to generate revenue. Bless the work of my hands. If it is your will for me to leave this relationship, give me wisdom and discernment on how to leave this abusive relationship in the safest way possible. Order my steps. Help me to trust in your ability to deliver, protect, and keep me. In Jesus's name, Amen.

Chapter 8: Our First Anniversary

September 2008

Everything seemed to be going right for us. Can you believe that we were even able to take a vacation on St. Simon's Island for a weekend? But Terrence became more withdrawn. He didn't seem like himself, and I couldn't understand what was going on with him. He was mad and snappy most of the time. The only time he seemed happy with me was when we were making love. All he did was work, shower, have sex, sleep, work, shower, have sex, and sleep on repeat.

My husband did not talk to me about his concerns. He felt that he should hold all that in and deal with it himself because "that's what a man does." It seemed that I only wrote in my diary when I was depressed or going through major difficulties. I knew I should write more often, but I didn't. Since nothing was going haywire in my life, I didn't write much. All of that was about to change...

When I heard him come in the door one evening, I got up from my seat at the computer table and flopped on the bed; I was excited about him coming up the steps.

I had practiced all day about how I was going to approach him about our anniversary. I wanted to go out of town, go to dinner, or something. We needed to do something romantic to celebrate our first year together.

As soon as he walked in the bedroom door, I jumped off the bed and threw my hands around his neck and hugged him close. He smelled of a mixture of tar and sweat when I leaned in to kiss him. He brushed me off like I was a fly or something.

"Stop," he snapped.

"Hey... baby."

"Hey," he replied rather dryly.

A little disappointed, I sat back down on the bed and asked, "Terrence, what are we going to do for our anniversary?"

"Nothing," he remarked. "It is just any other day." Terrence was looking harried and tired as he slid down into the chair at the computer table.

Tears welled up in my eyes. I chewed on my bottom lip. Indecision gripped me. I couldn't hold it in anymore. I began to cry. "Terrence, why would you say something like that?

"Uh! Stop crying! Yo ass is so got damn sensitive. You make such a big deal about days and holidays and birthdays! That shit ain't important. It just another day that the white man told ya'll niggas to celebrate and so there you go doing it."

I walked over to where he was sitting in the computer chair and put my hands softly on his shoulder as the tears streamed down my face at that point. He knocked my hand off his shoulder, rose to get up from the chair, and walked towards the bedroom door. "I gotta go."

I grabbed his shirt in an effort to plead my case with him. "Please don't leave. We need to talk about this."

I swung myself around to the stand between him and our bedroom door and blocked his exit with both of my hands touching near the top of the doorframe and my feet spreading to make an "X" of my body in the doorway.

"Terrence, why are you hurting me like this?"

"You hurtin' yourself. Get outta my way, Kim."

"No, Terrence. You will not run away from me. We need to talk about this.

"GET. OUT. OF. MY. WAY. KIM."

His face turned into something I had never seen before, but I didn't move. I picked up a white plastic hanger that was sitting on the dresser and began tapping him on the shoulder repeatedly with the hanger. He became obviously aggravated.

"Why are you saying stuff to hurt my feelings? Talk to me, Terrence."

"Kim, I said get the FUCK out of my way!"

When I refused to move, he backhanded me in the mouth so brutally that I fell down onto the floor...hard. Terrence looked back at me with an evil look and said, "I told you to get out of my damn way, didn't I? I bet you won't get in my damn way no mo."

I just sat on the floor, pulled my legs all the way up to my chest, and cried in shock and disbelief.

How could he do that to me?

Why would he say such awful things to me?

I was so confused. How could the man that could be so affectionate and loving towards me one minute act like a complete monster the next. I didn't know what to do.

He ran down the steps, out the door, and drove away.

When Terrence returned home, I was lying in the bed, curled up in the fetal position, with all the lights off. I hadn't accepted any calls, talked to anyone, or gone to pick up the children from my sister's house because I was too ashamed. He turned on the light and sat down on my side of the bed. "Sit up."

I slowly slid up until my back was against the cold backboard of the bed. He grabbed my face and kissed my lips softly. I flinched. Both of my lips were swollen, and the bottom lip, as well as the area around my chin, was bright red. My eyes were red and puffy from the multitude of tears I'd cried in the past three hours that he'd been gone.

"I'm sorry, baby. I was just mad, and I told you to get out of my way. When you kept tapping me, it made me mad. You don't ever hit a man."

I started crying and shaking my head. "I'm so sorry Terrence. I know I shouldn't have tapped you with that hanger."

I truly believed that it was my fault that he hit me. I was aggravating him; so, it was my fault, right?

"You hurt my feelings so badly, and I just wanted you to listen to me. And when you didn't, I wanted to get your attention. But my daddy beat my mama. and I can't stay with you if you hit me ever again. You've got to promise that you won't hit me ever again," I said.

"I promise," he said.

"No, that's not good enough. You've got to write it down and sign it like an agreement."

"What?!" he asked and began laughing.

"Stop laughing. It is not funny. You've got to write it down on a piece of paper that states that you will never hit me again and sign it. Right now."

"Okay. Gimme the paper." So, I handed him the paper, and he wrote:

"I, Terrence S. Roberson, promise never to hit my wife, Kimya, again. Signed, T.S.R."

And that was that. We kissed and made love all night long. Terrence kissed me on my face over and over again, carefully avoiding my swollen lips as the tears began to fall from my eyes.

He whispered in my ear over and over again that he was so, so, so sorry and would never do it again.

He lied...over and over again.

Chapter 9: Hot Grits and Hotter Tempers

October 17, 2008

In the weeks before our anniversary, Terrence found out he had sarcoidosis, which is the same thing his favorite comedian died from, and Terrence thought he was going to die too.

Sarcoidosis is a disease that causes inflammation in the lungs and lymph nodes. It caused him to have bouts of fever where he would sweat or have chills that only layers upon layers of clothing could relieve.

Just two weeks after hitting me, he broke his promise.

I prepared a breakfast for the family that included crisp bacon, sausage, scrambled eggs with cheese, grits, and hot buttered biscuits. I brought his plate up to him with a tall glass of Sunny Delight (one of his favorite drinks). He slowly sat up as I propped the pillow up behind him so he could eat. I kissed him on the cheek; he was burning up with fever.

"Baby, you want anything else?" I asked.

"Naw, I'm good."

Upon finishing, he laid back down on the pillows and turned over.

So, I took his plate downstairs and returned moments later with my first basket of clothes. I walked over to our bathroom, turned the light on, pulled the bathroom door up slightly so it wouldn't be so bright in the bedroom, and took my seat on the floor to begin folding. At this point, he was lying in our bed naked in the fetal position with the covers pulled over his head.

I got through half the basket when he said, "Go downstairs and fix me some mo' grits."

"Okay," I replied. "Gimme just a minute, baby. Let me finish this basket, and I will go downstairs and fix you some more."

"Bitch," he said, "take your ass downstairs RIGHT NOW and fix me some more God damn grits."

Startled, I dropped his shirt into the basket.

"Now, why are you talking to me like that, Terrence? I just asked you before I went downstairs if you wanted some more breakfast, and you told me you were full. I can fix you some more grits, but you need to say 'please' or something. You don't call me names and think that I'm going to go do what you say."

Terrence immediately jumped up from the bed, knocking over the basket of clothes. He swung the bedroom door open and ran downstairs to the kitchen. I ran behind him. I didn't know what he was going to do, and I was terrified.

"Terrence, please, baby. Terrence don't..."

He immediately began to open and slam all the cabinet doors and shouted, "Where are the bacon bits?!"

"I don't know."

He then looked at me with so much hatred in his eyes and said, "Well..., I. don't. want. these. then." Terrence snatched my pot of grits off the stove, took the top off, poured them in the middle of the floor, and dropped the pot with a loud clang.

"Now, bitch, clean that shit up."

He shoulder brushed past me, and he began stomping back up the stairs.

Tears of anger and hurt welled up in my eyes, and I yelled, "I'm not cleaning that up! You clean it up! Why would you do that? Terrence! Terrence! That is so childish. Clean it up."

Terrence went back into the room, got into bed, and pulled the covers over him as if nothing just happened.

I walked into the room and spoke again as calmly as I could with tears trickling down my face. "Terrence, you don't have to be here if you don't want to be. If I am making you that miserable, why don't you just go home to your parents?"

Silence.

His silence made me mad.

I was so angry and sick of his outbursts of rage toward Theron and me.

Sick of being called names.

Sick of being mistreated.

I mustered up more courage than I've ever had and walked toward the closet, took a deep breath, pulled three of his shirts off the rack, threw them to the floor, and asked him if he wanted me to help him pack. That was a mistake.

In an instant, Terrence leapt from the bed, throwing the covers to the floor, and charged me with both hands as if he were a linebacker and I were the running back with the football. My chest took the brunt of his hands as my body was forcefully shoved into the back of the closet. Bam! My head hit the wall.

"Don't fuck with me bitch or I will hurt you. Do you understand me?!" he said through clenched teeth as little drops of spit hit my face.

Then he let me go, and I fell to the floor. His mood switched to calmness as he casually walked back down stairs to the kitchen.

I rolled over to my knees and slowly stood up. My head was throbbing so badly. I reached into my hair and began to rub the spot that hit the wall and squinted hard. It hurt so bad just to touch it. I started crying hysterically, ran downstairs, grabbed my keys, and shouted that I was going to call the police. I ran out of the house in my bare feet, jumped in the car, and drove to Nichelle's house.

Upon reaching her house, I realized my phone was not with me. I ran to her door and wildly rang her doorbell. I hurriedly explained to Nichelle what happened. She invited me in and hugged me. Nichelle gave me some tissue and her phone to make the call to the police.

After calling, I thanked Nichelle for her help and walked back out to the car.

The events of the morning flashed through my mind.

What did I do wrong?

Should I have stopped folding clothes and just went to make his breakfast?

I mean he WAS sick.

Usually he didn't act like that.

Why would he hurt me like that?

Then I went back home to wait for the police.

When I walked into the door, I found my phone broken in several pieces on the kitchen counter and Terrence in the bed with the covers pulled over him, resting comfortably.

I walked back out to my car and sat in it and sobbed until the police arrived. Still barefoot, I walked them up to the door after giving a report. As we walked into the house, Terrence walked down the steps.

"Sir, did you tackle Mrs. Roberson and cause her head to hit the back of the closet door?"

Terrence told the police officer that he didn't know what I was talking about. We had a disagreement, but we did not fight. When the police officer did a walkthrough of my home, the grits had been magically cleaned, and there was no evidence of any altercation.

At that point, one of the police officers took me out onto the porch.

"Listen, we can't tell that there was any sort of altercation here. If you feel that you are in danger, the only thing I can tell you to do is to leave, go down to the courthouse, and take out a restraining order. Ma'am, I cannot make your husband leave. You report is unsubstantiated."

My face dropped, and I looked at him in defeat. "You want ME to leave? This is my home." I began to cry again. "I bought it before we were married. Why can't you make him leave?"

"It's marital property ma'am. That's the law."

Years after this incident, I found out Terrence told the other police officer that he was upset over the way I was raising Theron. He told him that there was nothing wrong with him, and I baby him too much.

"Theron is violent, and if he touches me, I will beat his ass," Terrence explained to the officer.

Terrence told the police officer about previous altercations between them, and he actually had the nerve to tell the police officer that he told my son without my knowledge that he would kill him if he ever tried anything. He then told the police officer that he was moving back to South Georgia.

He didn't go back to South Georgia, I had to stay somewhere else for the night, and the police officer never reported what Terrence said to someone who could have helped us.

Spotlight on Abuse-Law Enforcement:

No other agency has more contact with victims of domestic violence than law enforcement agencies. They have the capacity to greatly reduce the rate of domestic violence in their communities when they get yearly training on how to identify and successfully intervene in an active domestic violence situation. If you are in an active domestic violence situation, law enforcement should:

- **Treat the call as a life and death matter.** Even if you cancel the call, they must still respond accordingly.
- **Use a "no siren" protocol.** Use of lights and sirens can escalate the situation and may be unnecessary. They should take a careful examination of the property and listen for impending threats before announcing they've arrived on the scene. .
- **Use the buddy system**. Law enforcement should respond in pairs. This allows them to separate you and the abuser in order to allow you the freedom to speak about the incident without being influenced or coerced into lying. Additionally, it gives them the opportunity to locate and remove any possible firearms.
- **Collect evidence.** They are required to take pictures of you and/or your property to assess the damage. They may even use audio or video recordings of your statements whether or not there is an arrest made.

- **Conduct a risk assessment.** For well-trained organizations, a risk assessment is a must! At this point, they can help you develop a safety plan or put you in touch with domestic violence agencies to help you create one and obtain other resources you need.
- **Make a mandatory arrest.** In some cases, officers are required to arrest the perpetrator. This occurs if the officer witnesses the abuse or if there is clear, physical evidence that abuse occurred ("How Police are Trained, n.d.).

What can you do about it?

Colossians 3:19 Husbands, love your wives and don't be bitter toward them.

Beloved, God does not condone abuse. There are many scriptures that tell the husband to love his wife as his own body, be willing to die for her, and to live with her in an understanding way. Just know there is nothing you could do to ever deserve to be abused. So, while God CAN change your abusive partner, sometimes it is best to separate for a while so you can both get the help you need. Whether you decide to leave or go is totally up to you, but make a safety plan either way and seek help/advice from a domestic violence agency in your area.

Pray. Father God, place your angels of protection all around me and my family. Keep us safe from all hurt, harm and danger.. You can turn the king's heart in whatever direction you choose. So turn the heart of _____ towards you. Allow him to be humble. Do not allow the thoughts of violence, malice, anger, or murder to be stirred up where we live. Help me to be as shrewd as a serpent and harmless as a dove. Help me to recognize danger when it occurs and act accordingly. Let there be peace that passes all understanding. In Jesus's name, Amen.

Chapter 10: Temporary Protective Orders

Ashamed of what happened, I didn't want to call my boss and assistant principal. Domestic violence is child abuse, and I was so afraid I might lose my children. I was afraid I would lose my job, but I knew I couldn't take it anymore.

I couldn't watch him hit my son and feel powerless anymore. I refused to watch my daughter look at us with those big brown eyes with tears streaming down her face and beg us to stop. I couldn't do that anymore.

So, I told my boss and assistant principal what happened and took off from work the next day in order to go down to the district attorney's office.

I nervously walked into the county courthouse building, through the metal detectors, and stopped to talk to the two sheriffs at the other end of the scanner. A tall, light-skinned, older sheriff told me where I should go if I wanted a protective order

I felt like my shame was showing as I walked slowly to get into the elevator. I could not hold back my tears any longer as I pushed the button to go to the third floor.

When I walked through the glass and wooden door and up to the counter, a small , middle-aged, white lady with wire-rimmed glasses greeted me. I told her briefly why I was there, and she handed me a set of papers to complete and went back to her work at the desk.

My hand shook nervously as I answered the questions. The papers said that he couldn't call, email, send letters to, or otherwise contact the children or me; enter our home; and buy or possess a gun. It said I couldn't have contact with him either. I was actually scared about completing the information.

Would he be mad with me?

Would he want to hurt me because I told others what was going on in our house?

Despite him hurting me earlier, all I could think about was how HE would feel about this order. Although I completed the paperwork and it was served, I violated the order two weeks later.

I knew the papers said that he couldn't contact me, but it had been two weeks, and I had not heard from him. This was very confusing because part of me wanted to call him. Part of me knew that I shouldn't. I felt so stupid. How could I love a person that obviously did not love me?

How could I love a man that would hurt my son?

How could I love a man that would hit me with his hands and damage me with his words?

Minutes turned into hours and hours turned into days and days turned into weeks. I became more and more lonely and began to question if what he did was really all that bad. I mean he DID have sarcoidosis. Maybe I wasn't understanding enough. Maybe I should have just made him another plate of grits. I mean, wouldn't I be upset too if I found out I had a potentially deadly disease? And what about the woman over the support group at church? She told me that I WASN'T being abused. She said I needed to submit more.

Daily, I cried about him and the situation. When I couldn't take it anymore, I called him.

"Hi Terrence."

"Hey."

"I need to talk to you."

He didn't say anything..

"Terrence, I love you so much. I don't understand why all of that happened."

Silence.

"Why did you do that to me? You promised my grandfather and me that you would not hurt me. How can you say you love me and treat me like that?"

He told me he was sorry.

He told me he wouldn't do it again.

He told me he wanted his family back.

All I could think about was that Thanksgiving was coming up and I wanted my husband home with me. I thought we could just kiss, make love, make up, and all the violence would be behind us. So, we talked about our plan that we would share with the judge.

Terrence went to court, told the judge the same things he told me, and asked for counseling.

He told the judge he was sorry.

He told the judge he wouldn't do it again.

And he told the judge he wanted his family back.

The judge told him that he was not going to order counseling because if he made him go, it wouldn't be effective. So, Terrence told him he would go on his own. The judge dropped the order, Terrence came home, we had wild, explosive make-up sex, and we got along...for about two months.

Even though he promised that we would get some counseling together, we did not. Although he did not hit me, his verbal assaults were getting worse. He began calling me a bitch every other day like he was saying, "Pass the salt." It reminded me of things I would hear my dad say when I was a child. It was becoming more than I could bear.

Terrence was not working, and our bills were beginning to get behind again. His mood matched our declining finances. Instead of praying to God and asking for direction, he turned on us and shouted daily.

By February, Terrence and I got separated because he threw Mountain Dew on me while I was trying to sleep. I called his daddy and asked him to come and get him.

Terrence threatened me and told me that I was going to feel sorry about putting him out and for calling his father.. It seemed as though he was angry about having sarcoidosis, but he refused to go and get help for it.

On top of that, Corinne ruptured her eardrum, and my dad had fallen in his apartment and broke his pelvic and tail bones. I was feeling very overwhelmed, but I still trusted in the Lord.

After about a month, Terrence's dad called me and told me that he couldn't take it anymore and he was bringing Terrence home.

"Where is Terrence's home?" I asked

"Right there with you."

"Mr. Roberson, I don't know what to do with Terrence. He keeps hurting me."

"Ya'll are married and you are supposed to work it out. If he hurt you, just call me darling, ok?"

"Yes, sir. Where are you now?" I answered

And within thirty minutes of that conversation, they were dropping him off at my house and returning to Glenwood.

Immediately upon coming into our home, he began to terrorize me. He pushed me against the wall with his body and put his finger over my mouth in the dining room.

The children were upstairs.

"I told yo ass that you were going to regret calling my ma and dad, didn't I?

"Terrence..."

"Shut up, you stupid bitch!"

With tears trickling down my face, I begged him to please be quiet. I didn't want to let the kids know what was going on.

"I don't give a shit 'bout them hearing us. Now, fix my God damn dinner, and don't say nothin' else to me about it. I'll let you know what we gon' do in the morning."

Just then Corinne came downstairs; she had woken up from her afternoon nap. As soon as she heard his voice, she went running to him.

"Mr. Terrence! You're home!"

He scooped her up in his arms and gave her a kiss. "How's daddy's baby?"

"Mr. Terrence, eww, your hair is scratchy!" She started laughing and began to act like she was wiping his kisses off her face.

"How's my big girl?" he asked as he put her down.

She told him all the things that were going on in school since he had been gone.

I held back the tears that wanted to fall. I felt so torn. On the one hand, Corinne had a father in the house with her every day. He DID love her and showed it by bringing her with him to work, taking her on horseback and four-wheeler rides, and playing tea party with her. One time when he gave her a spanking, he cried more than she did. Right after it was over, he took her to the local Wal-Mart to buy a toy.

I really didn't know what to do about our marriage.

Right after dinner, Terrence went to bed, and when I tried to go and sleep on the couch, he demanded that I get into bed with him.

I tossed and turned most of the night and so did he. When I finally went to sleep, I woke up to him being inside me.

"Terrence, what are you doing?"
"What it feel like I'm doing? You my wife. I'm not yours. Don't question me. You not supposed to deny me. Ain't that what the Bible say?"

I closed my eyes and choked out a "yes."

I'd been here before. I just disconnected my body from my mind and allowed him to finish his business before he went back to sleep.

The next day, he informed me that I wasn't going to work. He told me that I would take "the baby" to school, and he would let me know where we would end up.

We just drove around for most of the day, and he repeatedly called me names, talked badly about my son, and told me he "could" poison us all if I ever called his family on him again. Even though I had my phone all day, he wouldn't allow me to make any phone calls.

Every time I questioned him about where we were going, he would say, "Just drive, bitch!"

That afternoon, there must have been some divine intervention because he ran a really high fever all day, and when the pain coursing through his body became too much to bear, he told me he needed to go to the hospital. I convinced him to let me take him to the VA.

After a series of tests, the doctors told him they were going to keep him, but he ripped the IVs out of his arms, demanded that I give him the car keys, and left the hospital.

The doctors asked me if I were afraid of him. I began to cry and affirmed what they already knew. The doctors had two police officers go out into the parking lot to get my keys from Terrence.

I left Terrence at the VA.

Within minutes of leaving the VA, he began calling me over and over. Frightened and confused, I didn't know what to do so I answered the phone.

"Hello."

"What the fuck did you leave me here for?" he shouted into the phone.

"You've been scaring me all day, Terrence. I'm scared of you and what you are going to do to me."

"Ain't nobody going to do nothing to yo crazy ass! You betta come back and get me right now!"

I hung up on him.

Terrence continued to call me repeatedly and asked me to come and get him. He told me that he would never forget what I did to him that day.

After a conversation with a relative, she convinced me not to leave him down there because he had nowhere to go. We made a plan to pack suitcases for my children and place them in the trunk. Kelly called her friend college friend, Jackie, and asked if the children and I could stay with her, and she agreed.

I picked up Andria and her mom, Betty, to ride with me to pick him up. I knew with Betty in the car, I would be safe. She was a no-nonsense, uncompromising woman that gave you the sense that you did not mess with her.

When we picked him up, his whole demeanor changed. He was nice and charming and carried on a very sweet conversation with us. I allowed him to take his things in the house and informed him that the children were at Andria's house. I needed to take Betty and Andria home, pick up the children, and I would be right back.

I didn't go back to the house with him.

Spotlight on Abuse: Why Doesn't She Just Leave:

Did you know, on average, women leave the abuser seven times before they give up on the relationship? Don't feel guilty if you have gone back and forth with him, Leaving or staying are completely your decision. If you know someone that is in an abusive relationship, you should never pressure her to "get out now!" Actually, if he THINKS she is leaving, if she ACTUALLY leaves, or within TWO YEARS of her leaving can be the most dangerous time for her. The abuser feels as if he is losing control and may do something to try to regain control. It may seem easy to just leave; however, there are barriers to her complete independence.

While the greatest barriers to leaving is feeling isolated and lack of access to financial resources, other barriers may include:

- **Batterer.** The batterer is famous, influential, or a celebrity and can afford to pressure your family, law enforcement, or members of the judicial system. The victim may feel that no one will believe her. The victim believes the batterer's threats that he will kill her and the children if they attempt to leave.
- **Children's best interests and/or pressure.** You may not want to take the children's other parent from them, especially if the children are not abused. Consequently, the children love their other parent and may try to make you feel guilty about leaving the other parent.

- **Cultural, gender, religious, and racial Differences.** "Norms" of how certain races should handle things (i.e. the strong black woman stigma) and/or feelings of not being treated fairly by the justice system (i.e. fear of being deported) can be barriers to leaving an abusive relationship.
- **Denial and/unsure of abuse.** Growing up in an abusive household or years of exposure to violence can desensitize you to the existence of danger. Sometimes you may believe that if you are a better partner (cooked and cleaned better, had sex more, gave more money, etc.), the abuse would stop and he would "go back" to the way he was.
- **Disabled and elderly.** Victims that are disabled or elderly are dependent on their abusers for care. If they challenge them, the abuser may restrict access to services.
- **Excuses.** Issues he may be facing can be used as a crutch for the abuse, such as job loss, money issues, alcoholism/drug abuse, job stress, and illness ("Obstacles," n.d.).

What can you do about it?

Joshua 1:9 Haven't I commanded you: be strong and courageous? Do not be afraid or discouraged, for the Lord your God is with you wherever you go."

God did not give you a spirit of fear. I cannot emphasize enough for you to contact a domestic violence advocate and create a safety plan, whether you decide to leave or go.

Pray: Father I thank you that you did not give me a spirit of fear. You gave me love, power, and soundness of mind. Teach me how to walk like someone who is affirmed and rooted in your faithfulness. Father God, give me wisdom, discernment, and resources for this season I am in. Please send me to the people I need to speak with about my situation and help me make the best decision for my family. In Jesus's name, Amen.

Chapter 11: Reconciliation?

Jackie's house provided space, peace, and the most restful sleep I'd had in a long time. After my children went to sleep every night, Jackie's guest bed lulled me to sleep after I cried and prayed. Although Jackie didn't know me well(she was Kelly's friend from college), she treated me with so much respect and dignity. She never judged me for my decisions and was always willing to pray with me, talk to me about God, watch Christian television, or just listen to me vent.

About three weeks into my stay, I had a conversation with Jackie about my relationship with Terrence. We talked about all the incidents: when he hit me in the mouth, tackled me in the closet, threw Mountain Dew on me, and beat Theron.

"Jackie, I am torn between loving him and not wanting him to hurt my son or feeling or looking stupid. He was so wonderful before we got married, but now it seems like everything has changed.

I went to my church for help and the ladies in the domestic violence support group said he wasn't abusing me. They said he was only acting like this because of the sarcoidosis and that I needed to give him more support."

"What do you believe?" Jackie asked.

"I don't know any more...I feel like if he went to the doctor and got help for the sarcoidosis, he would stop mistreating us."

"Kim, you are going to have to pray about it and ask God what to do. Only He can guide you in the right direction."

I threw my hands up in desperation. "I know you're right, Jackie, but this-is-just-SO-HARD!

Even throughout this process, I still wanted to believe in the power of love to win over Terrence. I spoke to him daily during the separation, but he never said anything that indicated he was sorry for his actions. Some days he was angry with me and would say hurtful things like how he would put antifreeze in my Kool-Aid and no one would ever know it. Other days he said that he missed me and wanted the children and me to come back home.

After thanking Jackie for her hospitality, I returned home in the first week of April 2009, when Terrence promised that he would go to the doctor to treat his sarcoidosis and go to counseling about his feelings about his illness and to fix our broken relationship. He told me that he couldn't do it alone, and I believed him.

"I need, you Kim. You supposed to be my wife. You supposed to help me. The Bible says you're my helpmate."

How could I argue with that? On the way home, listening to Alicia Keys' "No One," and I believed it would be the anthem for our reconciliation.

I wondered what my friends would think about my decision to go back.

Would they be mad?

Would they understand?

The answer to that would-be no. Some of my friends expressed how hurt they were with my decision to go back. They did not have the heart to go through it all over again... I didn't understand at the time that they weren't equipped to handle the abuse. They loved me, but they felt as though they needed to distance themselves from me in order to have some peace themselves.

Terrence kept part of his promise. He went to the doctor to treat his sarcoidosis, but he did not get counseling, but things seemed to go back to normal from April of 2009 through January of 2010. Terrence began taking the meds for the sarcoidosis, gained most of the ninety pounds back he lost, and even returned to work.

Surprisingly, the man I loved seemed to return. He would bring me flowers "just because." He would leave cards for me on my pillow when he went to work in the morning. And, at night, we continued to reconnect sexually with each other. Life was GREAT!

Christmas 2009 was the best holiday we'd shared with one another. Not only had he had a complete turnaround from sarcoidosis and went back to work, Theron was doing well in school and hadn't had any crisis situations in more than a year. Corinne was just happy that we were all getting along, and she had her Terrence Daddy back at home. It was a wonderful time!

I spent the entire month preparing the house for Christmas. I went to Michael's and Hobby Lobby to buy new ribbon to make bows for the entire house. Keeping myself busy was not hard at all as I spent many nights making a wreath for the front door, evergreen swags for the fireplace mantel, and huge burgundy bows for the windows.

I loved making the house beautiful for Christmas. Christmas music played nightly in our home, and my family couldn't come home one day without the smell of fresh baked chocolate chip cookies or snickerdoodles meeting them at the door. I even got Mr. Bah Humbug himself into the Christmas spirit that year.

"Terrence, how much do you love me?" I asked him one evening as he walked into the house from work.

He walked up to me, gave me a kiss, picked me up, spun me around, and started singing along to the song on my CD, "This Christmas, "by Donny Hathaway.

He put me down and started laughing. "What do you want woman?"

Pulling myself closer, I responded with a huge smile on my face. "Well, the children and I were wondering if you would put up the Christmas lights on the house this year? That would really make me happy." I smiled even wider.

Terrence just started laughing and said, "I'm only going to put up the lights if I can keep them up all year."

I immediately raised my right eyebrow in protest and placed my hands on my hips, "But..." Before I could get out my contradiction, he began laughing again and agreed to my request. He assured me that he would put the lights up before the weekend was over.

I went to bed that night thinking I was one lucky woman because my marriage appeared to be turning around. I didn't see a glimpse of the man that was here just last year. Those two men were so different that he even named them. "Terry" was the sweet, loving version of himself. "Terrence" was the mean, abusive version of himself. Well, Terrence was LONG gone.

Christmas Day was remarkable. The children woke up to a ton of presents that we provided all on our own!

Even though he told me not to buy him anything, I did anyway. I absolutely loved the way he smelled in cologne. It was just a little something I picked up from Walmart so I figured he would not mind.

After the kids and Terrence opened their presents, Corinne, dressed in blue Cinderella pajamas, slid between Terrence and me on the sofa and gave me the present she bought at the Santa Workshop at school. It was wrapped in beautiful blue and white snowman paper with a white bow on it. My little girl was always going to make sure that she gave a present to me. She smiled the sweetest smile ever and handed it to me with pride. Inside was a red and black oven mitt.

"Mommy, now you have one to go on both hands and you won't burn your hands anymore."

"Thank you, Rinny Coo-Coo. I LOVE it!"

Last year she bought me one and so she wanted to buy me another one to fit on my other hand. She gave me a huge hug, and I kissed her sweet cheek.

I immediately took it into the kitchen to use as I prepared a huge Christmas breakfast which consisted of cinnamon and vanilla French toast, fluffy pancakes, our favorite homemade butter pecan syrup, bacon, and Corinne's favorite omelets with Colby jack cheese, mushrooms, green peppers, and onions.

Right after breakfast, I sank down into the couch, exhausted from being up all night wrapping presents, making love, and waking up early to make breakfast. I told the children to begin to pick up their wrapping-paper trash.

Terrence told me that he had a present for me. I wasn't expecting one at all. Earlier, when the children were opening their presents, I didn't ask him for mine. I already had the best present ever—my family was perfect again.

"I didn't see anything under that tree. Stop playin', Terrence."

"It's under there, woman. Go back and look."

I looked under the right side of the tree. There was nothing there.

"You're getting closer." He started laughing.

Theron, dressed in his red, white, and blue Superman PJs got in on the action and began trying to look for it, too.

I walked past the mixture of torn Santa Claus, Barbie, and Spiderman wrapping paper to the left side of the tree. Nothing.

"Nope. You cold now," he teased.

I started laughing at this point and put my hand on my hip. "Terrence Sherod Roberson, stop playing with me right now. There is no present under this tree."

"Did I tell you that it was under the tree?" He squinted and began scratching his head. "Keep looking, woman!" He was laughing so much that he almost fell off the step where he was standing.

The more I looked around the tree, the more he laughed. Finally, I caught sight of a little golden bronze bag beside the leather chair with the word "Jared" written across it.

I screamed and ran over to the bag. My heart started beating so fast...I almost couldn't catch my breath. "You went to Jared? How could you afford to do that?" I said as I sat down in a chair.

He started walking toward me with the world's largest grin on his face.

I reached my hand into the bag, pulled out the little cream-colored box, and opened it. My hands were shaking.

Tears of joy started rolling down my face when I saw the most beautiful diamond ring nestled in that perfect little box. It was so pretty that I didn't even want to take it out the box. I just held it and watched how the light glimmered through the tiny diamond clusters.

"Are you gone take it out the box, woman? I got you white gold like you said you wanted."

I placed it on my finger with pride. It was the most beautiful, piece of love wrapped around my finger that I had ever seen.

I immediately jumped up and kissed him. The children made vomit sounds and groans of protest, but I didn't care.

I whispered in his ear about how much I loved the ring. "Now let me go upstairs and thank you properly, Mr. Roberson."

Making love always seemed to make things better between us. It was the way we celebrated AND covered up things.

While lying in his arms, he kissed me on my forehead and said, "I love you, Kim. I-love-you. I promise that things are going to be better from now on. You will never see Terrence again. Terry is the man you fell in love with, the one from Glenwood, the one that knows how to treat you."

I fell asleep in his arms feeling safe, reassured, and happy. I believed him and felt that I could finally exhale.

I was wrong.

Spotlight on Abuse - Cycle of Violence:

If you are in the middle of an abusive relationship, you are probably experiencing mixed emotions. On the one hand, you love him; on the other hand, you think about leaving often due to explosive episodes. How can he be so sweet, kind, loving, and generous one moment and then blow up at you at other times? Wouldn't it all be so simple if he would just go back to being the person he was before? His actions are following the cycle of abuse.

- **Tension Building Phase:** During this period, the victim begins to feel as if she is walking on eggshells or walking a tightrope in order to keep the abuser from exploding. The abuser is holding in large amounts of anger and tension. The victim works hard at being the best partner possible (cooking, cleaning, having sex, keeping the kids quiet, etc.) to prevent a potential blow-up. This is the longest phase.

- **Explosion Phase:** In this phase, all the anger and tension comes to a head and results in an emotional, physical, verbal, and/or sexual assault. This attack can scare both the victim and the abuser; consequently, they will place the blame on other things (drugs, alcohol, being stressed, etc.) or act as if the situation never occurred in the first place.

- **Honeymoon Phase:** In the beginning of the relationship, your partner puts his best foot forward. Positive feelings are felt on both sides. You may feel as if your partner is perfect. After an explosion, your partner will be very apologetic and humble. This is the candy, flowers, and cards stage. Your significant other is very loving during this period; however with each explosive episode, the honeymoon period gets shorter and shorter. When the honeymoon ends, the couple goes right back into the tension phase and continues until someone breaks the cycle ("Cycle of Violence," n.d.)

What can you do about it?

Proverbs 22:24-25 "Don't make friends with an angry man,[a]and don't be a companion of a hot-tempered man, or you will learn his ways and entangle yourself in a snare."

The scripture says it all. Sometimes it is best to speak with an advocate, make a safety plan, and leave. You didn't say or do something to "set off" the abuser. His anger has nothing to do with you.. Since you didn't create how he responds to anger, you can't control it. It is not your job alone to maintain happiness and peace in your relationship. Your relationship should be mutually satisfying.

You cannot save your partner and if he really wanted help, he would work towards getting healthy on their own. If you choose to stay with you're a partner at this time, ask an advocate about joining a good support group in your area.

Pray: Father God, please help _____ recognize that anger is not a sin, but how he handles his anger is the problem. Help me to see the abuse is not my fault. Help me to recognize the signs of impending danger. Lord, be my way of escape in troubled times. In Jesus's name, Amen.

Chapter 12: The Beginning of the End

January 2010

I had not been going to church since November and felt myself slipping more and more from God and anything that had any resemblance of the church. I did not understand why, but the more Terrence told me that he hated my church and my pastor, the more I stayed away. Things were going so well; I didn't want to rock the boat.

On Martin Luther King Jr. Day, I sat on my comfy, brown couch in my favorite pink, flannel pajamas. I was glued to my television; I was watching the Martin Luther King Jr. Day special. Susan L. Taylor, former editor of Essence magazine had my heart in her hands as she spoke about how Coretta loved Dr. King in her opening address.

Taylor explained how Coretta Scott King told her how important Dr. King always made her feel despite his great presence in the world.

I imagined how it would feel for Terrence to feel that way about me. How it would feel for him to think what I said, thought, or did was important. How it would feel for him to truly value me.

My thoughts were soon interrupted by the telephone ringing.

"Hello."

"Hey, Kim. Whatcha doing?"

It was Kelly. She always seemed to call me at the right moment. Sometimes I would joke that she had my phone tapped.

"Girl, I am looking at the Dr. King celebration. It is sooooo good." I told her.

"I know I was watching it, too," Kelly said. "Listen, since you haven't been to church, I wanted you to know that Bishop has called a fast for the year."

She was always on fire for God, and she told me of the ways that this fast could change my situation if I trusted God to do it. I got really excited after talking to her and made up my mind to do it too.

We didn't have much money to purchase food for the fast because ideally I would have liked to do a Daniel fast where I consumed only fruits and vegetables for the specified period of time; however, I went with cutting out all sweets and salty snacks from my diet (which is EXTREMELY hard for me).

I ran upstairs to get my journal, leaving the television on in the living room. I flopped down on my bed with my favorite pen and purple journal with an island scene on it (given to me by my student and her mom last year during Teacher Appreciation week).

I quickly made a list of all the things I wanted God to do for me and my family during the fast:

1. Heal Theron of all that is afflicting him,
2. Deliver Terrence from cigarettes,
3. Heal Corinne of enuresis,
4. Give us a financial breakthrough to pay all debts past and present,
5. Strengthen my marriage, and
6. Strengthen our (Terrence's and my) bond with the children.

I wanted the year to be a year of joy, love, peace, health, and overflow of wealth so we could get out of debt and help others.

As soon as the fast started, I began to experience problems.

The number one problem was a lack of money. While I was thankful that for the first time in a long time, our family seemed to be at peace, we still had no money. At the time, I remember not having lunch money for the children or gas money to get back and forth to work. Corinne was going to after-school care, and I didn't even have the money to pay them. Coming home by herself was definitely not an option. So, what was I going to do?

I found myself getting increasingly angry with God, and I couldn't figure out why He was allowing these things to happen when I was taught that the Lord knew what I was in need of before I could ask or even think of it.

My bills were out of control. On top of that, my dad needed medical supplies at the personal care home where he was living, and the pharmacy that filled his prescriptions started sending me collection letters. They wouldn't supply any more of his medication until I paid the bill! It seemed as though that godly principle wasn't applying to me at that point.

To make matters worse, Terrence was getting sick again. He began smoking cigarettes again in August of 2009 against his doctor's orders and was now beginning to complain about being sick. He wouldn't go to the doctor or call in about another prescription. Why were we going backward?

Diary Entry:

"Lord, I feel abandoned by you today. Why does it seem as though we have taken great strides forward only to take great strides back?"

Terrence began slowly sinking back into his "cave." Some days he would get up and go to work, but some days he would simply lie in the bed with his curtains drawn. He told me that the black birds kept circling our home because they smelled death. He kept saying that he was going to die. He seemed to be fixated on his own death.

I couldn't understand why this was happening because I fasted LAST year about healing Terrence, and I was so angry with God because I felt that He had only given him a temporary healing. At the same time, I was afraid of this because I knew that when Terrence got sick, whether it was a headache, cold, or sarcoidosis, he would begin to show his angry side again, and nobody liked to see Terrence when he got angry.

I begged God to help me. But it seemed as though He wasn't listening.

The more we went without money, the more frustrated I got. Our utilities were getting disconnected, and we did not have any food.

One day I was so angry with Terrence that I declared that we would not be together much longer. He had begun to call me names again and treating us harshly. I began to retaliate verbally and that wasn't in my character at all. Because I was so upset most of the time, I began to take out my frustrations on Theron and Corinne as well, which manifested into me snapping at them for every little thing they did.

No sooner than the fast was over did the bottom drop out of our marriage.

One Saturday morning, I awoke to the sweet sounds of Terrence sleeping. I decided to go downstairs, make him breakfast, and bring it back to him in bed so that he would start his morning off on the right foot—without any arguments. I tiptoed into Theron's room first and kissed him on the forehead while he was sleeping.

I then tiptoed into Corinne's room and stepped on one of her Barbie dolls. "Ouch," I said.

She looked up at me and groaned. "Good morning, Mommy."

"Good morning, Rinny." I kissed her on the cheek, and she rolled over to go back to sleep.

Downstairs, I sang along to "Close to You" by Bebe and Cece Winans and prepared our breakfast. I carefully measured the White Lily flour into the large aluminum bowl, mashed the cold chunks of butter with my fork in the flour, and poured the cold buttermilk to make the dough for my famous homemade biscuits.

After putting the rolled biscuits into the oven, I placed my large frying pan on the stove and put the thick, Applewood bacon in the pan for frying. The smell of bacon was so sweet and inviting; it was sure to get my little princess out of bed. And I was right!

It wasn't long before she came downstairs. She loved to come watch and help me cook. She was always the first one up in the morning.

"Mommy, can I help?"

"Wash your hands first and sing the ABC song to make sure your hands are really clean."

I told her to get the pan for the grits and get the cheese and another stick of butter out of the fridge.

When we finished cooking, I sent her upstairs to get T.J. and Terrence for breakfast. Terrence refused, as I thought he would, but T.J. came down. After T.J. and Corinne said the grace with their own rendition of "God is great, God is good," we enjoyed breakfast.

I joked with them for a while, turned on the television, and took my husband's breakfast with a cup of fresh brewed coffee upstairs to him in bed.

He sat straight up in the bed and gratefully devoured all of the food. He told me that he wasn't feeling very well, but he did not hesitate to properly thank me for the wonderful breakfast I'd just provided for him. He was NEVER too sick for that.

We made love over and over again that morning until late in the afternoon. I got up while he was still sleeping so that I could shower and take my son out for our monthly date.

Every month, I would switch and take my children out for a date. This month was Theron's turn. The previous month, I had taken Corinne to the American Girl Store at North Point Mall and had lunch with her.

On this day, I promised Theron that I would take him to see that new *Avatar* movie with Zoe Saldana.

I sat down on the bed after dressing and gave Terrence a kiss on the lips.

"Mmm, you smell good. Where you going?" he asked.

"Baby, remember I told you that I was going to take Theron on a date today to see Avatar? We are going to eat at Steak and Shake and then go see the movie. You want anything before I go?"

"You want Big Daddy to give you more lovin' before you leave?"

"No, Terrence," I said giggling like a schoolgirl. "I will see YOU when I get back, and I will see what I can do about that 'lovin' when I get back."

He smacked me on the bottom, turned over, and went back to sleep. I took Corinne to Sandy's house and Theron and I went to see *Avatar*.

We had an awesome time during our date. We picked up Corinne from Sandy's house and got back in the car to go home.

"Mommy."

"Yes, Corinne."

"My tummy hurts. I have been going to the bathroom over and over again at Auntie Sandy's house."

I knew what that meant. Several of the students at my school had a stomach virus. It was going around. Theron began complaining that his stomach hurt as well (though his was probably due to all the junk he just had on our date—a hamburger, fries, a milkshake, popcorn, and candy). When we got home, they both raced to the bathroom.

I noticed Theron's shoes were in the middle of the floor in the living room so I shouted for him to pick them up as I walked upstairs so I could take off my shoes and change clothes.

As soon as I walked in the bedroom door, Terrence, who was in the same spot in bed as he was before I left, asked, "Anybody take out the damn dog when ya'll got back?"

"No, baby. I will take him as soon as I use the bathroom."

"Why can't one of them chillun' take him out NOW?"

I could tell from his tone of voice that he was very agitated. I became increasingly uneasy at his reaction.

"Terrence, they are both sick. I think they both are coming down with that stomach bug..."

"Then why can't you take his ass out right now! He been barkin' all fuckin' day, and I couldn't sleep. One day y'all gon' come home and that damn dog gon' be dead or gone."

"Terrence, now wait a minute. You don't have to..." My uneasiness had switched to anger. I was tired of his rants, shouts, and bullying us.

"Bitch, I said take that dog out right now!"

"Terrence..."

He jumped out of bed, still naked from the morning, went to the door, and shouted, "One of y'all need to take that damn dog out right now befo' I throw him out the doe'." He then slammed the bedroom door.

At this point, I stood up. "Now wait a minute. Don't you talk to them like that!"

"Bitch, I'll say whatever the fuck I wanna say. I am the man round here.

"Don't call me a bitch again."

He walked slowly over to me, pushed me hard, raised his eyebrows, and said, "Bitch."

I pushed him with both of my hands into the dresser, and it rocked against the wall. I shouted, "I said don't call me a bitch no fucking more! And don't you put your hands on me no motherfucking more!" I had had enough.

He looked stunned.

Just then, my son opened the door to my bedroom with his black shoes in his hands and pleaded, "Come on, guys. Terrence, please don't hit my mom anymore, and Mom..."

Before he could finish, Terrence pushed him out the door and into the hall. He began punching my son like some kind of raving maniac. Theron fell down in the hallway, and Terrence began kicking him all over his body.

At that point, Corinne came out of her bedroom and started screaming, "Get off my brother! Get off my brother!"

I told her to go to the neighbor's house to call the police. She went down the steps and out the front door.

I grabbed Terrence around the waist and managed to pull him off Theron long enough for my son to run out the house.

The shouting and screaming between us escalated until the police arrived. Corinne was unable to call the police because she was very frightened and she loved Terrence and her brother very much. She was torn about what to do. Theron was the one to make the call.

Once again, Terrence denied the fight and did so very calmly. The sheriff knew something wasn't right. He noticed a small cut, maybe the size of a popped pimple, under my son's eye and asked me if Terrence had done it.

Terrence looked at me.

I wasn't going to be intimidated anymore.

He wasn't going to hurt me or my children anymore.

"Yes, sir. Terrence did that to him." I told the officer the whole story. They read him his rights, handcuffed him, and took him away.

After I comforted the children and sent them to bed, I sat in the empty bathtub, allowing the steady, hot flow of water from the shower to fall on my body. I sobbed loudly.

"Jesus! I need you! This is not what I asked for!" Al Green's "How Can You Mend a Broken Heart?" was playing in the background.

I felt like a loser. I felt like the words of that song. I was so broken.

Why did Terrence do that to T.J.? How could I have let this happen? I pulled my legs into the fetal position and wanted to just disappear.

After that incident, Terrence and I would never live together again.

Spotlight on Abuse-Spiritual Abuse:

Spiritual abuse can occur when one partner repeatedly uses his actions to control the other partner's relationship with God and interactions with the place of worship. In addition to power and control, guilt and manipulation are added to the tools used to emotionally abuse you. You may feel like your partner uses religion as a basis to establish supremacy over you. Specifically, he may use the scriptures or sacred texts dealing with "submissiveness" to hold you in bondage. It can include:

- Ridiculing/insulting your religious beliefs and/or spiritual leaders
- Preventing you from attending services
- Preventing you from tithing or giving to the church
- Using sacred texts to control, manipulate, or justify abuse
- Forcing you to raise your children according to one faith or no faith at all ("Spiritual Abuse," 2015).

What can you do about it?

John 8:32 "You will know the truth, and the truth will set you free."

You should speak with a leader in your house of faith, create an emotional safety plan, and look for ways to express your faith safely. If your clergy member suggests couples counseling, don't do it! It can create a bigger problem. Abuse is not a couples' problem; it is an "abuser" issue only!

Pray: Father God, teach me your ways through your Holy Scriptures. Open up my eyes to be able to interpret them as you intended. Do not allow _____ to use the scriptures to oppress or control me. If I am in the wrong place of worship, lead me to my Earthly shepherd. Help me to know the truth about my relationship with _____ and my relationship with you. In Jesus's name, Amen.

Chapter 13: Discovering Love...Again

I met Michael through a mutual friend many years ago. We met again, hung out, and fell in love when I went on a family vacation in Savannah in July 2011. I didn't intend it, and I even tried to run from it. After eighteen months of separation and failed attempts at reconciliation and counseling with Terrence, I was growing increasingly low and depressed. All I knew was that for the first time in a long time, I felt free. I didn't know my life was about to change—for the worst and for the better—all at the same time.

Michael was a dark-skinned man of average height, who was two years older than me. He always smelled and looked like freshly starched and ironed linens on a Sunday morning. He had a smile that could melt my heart.

We all decided to drive to Savannah and hang out together on River Street the night before my vacation was due to end and I was to return home.

The street was bustling with excitement when we made it there. The incredible history of the area—with its century old cotton warehouses turned into antique shops, restaurants, and night spots—made the place beautiful; it was a place right out of some love story.

The smell of the cream, sugar, butter, and pecans drew us into Savannah Sweets. Corinne's favorite thing to do was to go into one door, get a sample of the pralines, go out the door of the other side of the store, and do it all over again. Silly girl. She convinced her brother to go along with her schemes. They probably did it five times before the employees realized what they were doing.

Theron and Corinne both saw the adults were going into Wet Willies and decided they wanted one of THOSE too.

"Mom, I want a slushy like that," Theron whined and pointed to Michael's drink.

"THAT is not a slushy, T.J. It has alcohol in it."

Theron noticed that there were two children sitting on the cobblestone road in front of the store with a plastic cup emblazoned with the logo from Wet Willies.

"Well, how did THEY get one then?" he said, pointing in their general direction.

I shrugged my shoulders, walked into the store, and purchased two nonalcoholic cups for them and one Monkey Shine for me. We walked back to the brick wall to sit down where everyone else was already seated and [11]talking junk or people watching.

---

[11] Ridiculing each other in a playful manner; playful banter

Michael sat on the right of me. I just sat and listened to the harmonies of the ships coming in and out of port and the live music playing. My moment was interrupted briefly by Michael and his friend arguing about whose turn it was to buy the next round of drinks.

Since I just finished my piña colada, I slid $20 into Michael's hand and said, "When you get up to go, will you bring me back another Monkey Shine? Cuz I already know who's gonna win THIS argument."

He stopped arguing long enough to look at me and say, "Why don't you come with me?"

So, I got up, smoothed my dress, and walked with him across the street. We laughed over his endless jokes. When we reached Wet Willies, we both ordered our drinks and paid for them. Just as we were heading out of the door, he turned and surprised me with a question.

With his head cocked to one side in his smooth, [12]swag on ten, kind of way, he said, "So, Motley, when you gonna let me take you out?"

I smiled at how he was looking at me. Everything inside me should have said that we couldn't go out, but what came out of my mouth was: "When do you want to?"

I was quite surprised by the answer I gave him. I never tell men that I would date them because I thought I should be divorced before I even THOUGHT about dating anyone else, but Michael was different.

---

[12] really cool, suave, or debonair manner

I saw him as being someone cool. We had been at the same parties before. I remembered that he made fun of the way I played Spades. This wouldn't be a date. I had convinced myself that this was more like hanging out.

"Why don't you come back down in two weeks?" he asked.

That's when my senses came back to me. "Don't you know I'm married?"

"I'm not trying to hang out with your husband. Just you."

I laughed and agreed to come back. This would definitely mark the turning point in my life for good.

Later that night, I had a "come to Jesus meeting" with Michael and his friends after being questioned over and over about why I was staying with my husband after the things people had heard about him.

So, after someone from our table discussion hit their hand on the table, got in my face, and said, "You're afraid of him, aren't you?"

I had to admit I was.

I left him and got back together with him four times over the course of our marriage. He never changed. He would be nice for a while and go back to hurting me again.

The emotional assaults and threats only got worse every time I mentioned divorce.

I had not moved forward with divorce because I was afraid Corinne would not have a father. He was really good to her.

I was afraid of displeasing God. He hated divorce.

I was afraid of looking like a failure—again.

I was afraid he might try to beat me up.

I was afraid Corinne would lose her father-daughter relationship with him.

All of a sudden, reality hit me in my face. I decided to leave Terrence for good. I was TIRED of being afraid. And being tired was worth more than being afraid.

I was tired of watching my children cry.

I was tired of being in debt because of the games he kept playing with my bank account.

I was tired of being silent about all the pain the kids and I were in.

I would not be afraid anymore. If God be for me, who dare stand against me, right?

Michael would protect me. Besides that, he told me over late-night drinks and conversation that he would.

July twenty-ninth could not arrive fast enough. I had been talking to Michael during breaks at school, lunch, planning period, after school, and every night on the phone. He was like a breath of fresh air.

In the two weeks since I made my decision about finally getting a divorce, Terrence began texting and calling me repeatedly. It was never-ending; this time, it seemed to be escalating.

On the ride to Savannah to hang out with Michael, I counted over ninety texts.

Terrence would text:

"A"

"B"

"C"

He would text all the way to "Z," and then he would begin with numbers. I thought this behavior was annoying but nothing to be alarmed about.

All I could think about was Michael and seeing him again and our first date. It took my mind off Terrence's escalating behavior.

When we arrived, I decided that I would be staying at Michael's house. He and I had already spoken about not having sex, so I wasn't worried about him [13]trying to get my cookies.

We were all going to hang out at Wet Willies that night—Michael, his two friends, and me. The moment he walked into the door at Wet Willies, wearing a freshly-starched, red Polo shirt and shorts, I felt a huge load lift off of me. I felt as though I could finally exhale. I have no idea what we all talked about that night in the restaurant…no idea at all. I was just waiting to go back to his house so I could feel warm, secure, and safe.

As we said our goodbyes to everyone, I put my bags into Michael's convertible black Benz and enjoyed the ride all the way to his house.

It was immaculate. I have never known a man to be so neat, clean, and orderly.

He showed me to my room. "You can sleep in here in the guest room."

"Ok. Don't be trying to sneak in here while I am sleeping and try any funny business, mister."

"Girl, don't nobody want to come in here with you." He started laughing. "Don't YOU try to sneak in my room with me."

---

[13] trying to have sex with a female

After he put my bags down, we went back into the living room and made jokes about the food (or lack thereof) in his refrigerator and talked for a few more hours before I went to bed.

Untouched. Happy. Warm. Secure. Safe. And at peace...for once in a long, long time.

The next morning, I woke up before Michael and began working on some stuff for school on my computer. I heard him get up some time later, talking to his friend on the phone as his friend, Jason teased him about me spending the night over there and how he wasn't going to get any of my cookies. He didn't seem bothered at all. That made me feel like he was proud to be with me.

Michael later came into the room after his conversation was over and kissed me on the forehead. That was it! I was in love. The forehead kiss does it every time.

"Get up, girl. We got shit to do!" he started laughing

"What?" I started laughing too.

We needed to get up and get started if we were going to go shopping and get lunch before it got too late.

We went to the outlets in Savannah to look for shoes for Theron and Corinne. I went into the Nike outlet and bought some pink and blue Air Jordans for Corinne, but I was unable to find shoes in T.J.'s size—he wore a fourteen. So, we decided to go and grab some lunch in the little mom and pop restaurant around the corner.

As we sat and talked, we eventually lingered on the topic of sex. After having just finished reading Steve Harvey's *Act Like a Lady, Think Like a Man*, I told him that we should wait ninety days. I didn't feel strong enough to tell him that we should wait until marriage because I liked him so much and falsely believed that men wouldn't want you unless you slept with them. Having been molested as a child and raped as a teen, I had established the belief that all that men wanted from you is sex.

"Do I have to wait WITH you?" he responded.

"Well, what does that mean?"

"It means, do I have to wait just cuz you're waiting? I mean, I won't try to have sex with you or nothing, but do I have to not have sex? Like at all?"

It was at this point that I realized what he was trying to say and I would have to compromise. I wanted him. Needed him. I knew what I would have to do to keep him.

I played it off by laughing and saying, "Yes, dude! You have to wait with me."

Michael started laughing too, but it was one of those "yeah, right" kind of laughs. I was not sure if he were serious or not. I felt like I had to have sex eventually, but today was not going to be the day. He already said he wasn't going to even try to do it.

Upon leaving the restaurant, I saw the Coach outlet.
I started jumping up and down and clapping my hands like
one of the four-year-olds I taught. (Hey, I taught Pre-K. I
was supposed to act like that.) So immediately we walked
in for browsing. The prices were incredible, and
immediately I opted for a brown signature bag with a pink
strap. Pink AND Coach? Who could resist?

I put my purchase up on the counter and reached
into my wallet for my card. Michael walked up behind me
and reached past my face to hand the cashier HIS card.

WHAT??? I turned around to face him in disbelief.

"What are you doing, Michael?"

"I just believe that you should have what you want. I
probably shouldn't, but I believe in spoiling my woman."

I walked out of that store and out of Savannah the
next day floating on a cloud.

Still untouched. Still warm. Still safe. Still secure.

God had sent me the man of my dreams – at last. I
learned that I could feel happy again. I could feel alive
again. I could feel safe again. But, I was relying on another
man to make me feel whole…again.

Chapter 14: Escalation Of Anger

August 2011

Upon coming home, I was growing increasingly fearful because Terrence's behaviors seemed very erratic. I knew he still had a key to my house and the passcode to my alarm system (because I could not change the locks according to the Temporary Protective Order. That did not make me feel secure. I made an appointment with ADT to change my alarm system anyway).

Imagine my surprise when I returned home from work at 3:30 on the day of my appointment, opened the front door, and found Terrence's belongings lying in the center of the living room floor and HIM, sitting on top of the dishwasher he purchased a long time ago. I immediately turned around and began walking fast towards Miyoshi's house.

Terrence ran out of the house and shouted that we needed to talk.

I shouted back: "No." I began walking faster towards Miyoshi's house—all the while praying that someone would be there.

Because he still had the key, Terrence jumped into my car and began following me up the street. Imagine my relief when I saw Harry coming out of the house at the same time as I arrived at the house.

He walked toward me, raising his palms towards the sky, and asked, "Now, what's going on here?"

I started desperately mouthing the words that I needed help, but before I could get Harry to understand me, Terrence immediately jumped out of the car, stood right next to me, and began asking me to come back down to the house so he could talk to me.

I held both hands toward him in a stop motion.

"No, Terrence. We can talk right here in front of Miyoshi's house. Right in front of Harry."

I was afraid he was going to hit me. I told him that if I went back with him to the house, he would try to do something to me.

He stepped closer and put his face inches from mine. If I want to do something to your ass, I will do it right here in front of Harry." I began slowly backing away from him, and he continued to walk toward me.

Harry quickly responded. "No, you won't hit her in front of me."

Terrence turned towards Harry and said, "Oh yes, I will."

"Oh, hell naw you won't. Now you won't be doing nothing to this woman. Not while I'm around. Now Terrence you know better than that."

Terrence slowly turned back to me. His whole tone had changed. He now spoke to me in a calm, easy voice. "Come on back to the house. I just want to talk to you. Harry can come on down to the house, too." He said as he looked at him out of the corner of his eye.

Harry quickly answered, "Terrence, I ain't going no damn where. You know good and well that I ain't going down to that house. Ain't no telling what you might do. Now, you can talk to her right here."

Terrence ignored Harry and asked one final time if I would go with him down to the house. Since I refused to follow, he began acting very erratically. He took his cell phone, broke the earpiece off, and threw both pieces to the ground.

"I'm going to call the police on you. You aren't even supposed to be here!"

He said that he didn't care and jumped back into my car. "You ain't seen nothing yet!" he said and drove off, leaving me without a car.

The sheriff arrived soon after he left and I began to describe what happened. I told him that we had an order of protection because of the incident that happened with my son over a year ago.

After calling into dispatch, Sheriff Botsky informed me that we did not have a protection order in place; instead we were issued a non-violent contact order which meant Terrence was able to come to our home and take my car because it was marital property.

I grabbed Sheriff Botsky's uniform and began crying loudly. "If you don't help me, he is going to hurt me!"

"Well that's your fault!" he shouted back and pushed me off him. "Why didn't you get a divorce?"

"I don't have the money to get an attorney. How am I going to get a divorce?"

Sheriff Botsky told me that all I had to do was go down to the courthouse, file a new order of protection, and pay $200 for a divorce and complete the paperwork myself.

Right after school the next day, my coworker and friend, Jackie Legare drove with me to the District Attorney's office to try to get an order of protection.

The lady sitting behind the desk used both hands to push her little rolling chair out from behind the desk. She walked up to the window.

"May I help you?"

"Yes, I need to get a protection order. My husband broke.."

"You got an address?"

"No. I don't know where he is. He supposed to be stayin..."

"I can't help you without an address, hon."

And with that, she walked back to her desk, sat down, looked at her computer, and began typing.

I walked away feeling hopeless.

That afternoon, my sister took me to pick up Corinne from her daycare center to talk to Ms. Pearl, the afternoon manager.

Corinne was out on the playground playing with her friends. I watched her for a minute from the parking lot. She hadn't noticed that I was there yet. She was running around, laughing, and playing tag. Corinne had no idea what was going on.

I walked into the office and was greeted by Ms. Pearl. She always had such a warm smile and made people feel like a million dollars every time you were in her presence.

"Hey, Miss Kimya. How was school today?" She asked as she sprayed a bright blue liquid onto the table and began wiping it off.

"Hi, Ms. Pearl. May I talk to you a minute?" She immediately stopped cleaning and motioned for me to follow her into the other room.

"Sure, come on in here, and have a seat."

"Ms. Pearl, I want to take Terrence's name off all of Corinne's papers. I do not want him to be able to pick her up from school."

"Why, Miss Kimya?"

"He has been acting crazy and I don't know what to do." I put my face in my hands and began crying. "I may have to take Corinne out of her school and aftercare. He has stolen my car, broke into my home, and he may try to take her from me to hurt me or something."

"Miss Kimya, we cannot do that without legal papers. He is her father."

I shook my head in disagreement. I explained to her that he was her stepfather, and there was not a legal document in place granting custody. She told me that she would obtain permission from the owners to ensure she was in compliance with the law. I told her that I would be back to change the paperwork.

By the end of the week, after several correspondences with Terrence, I told him that I filed a stolen car report, and if he were caught in it, he would go to jail. He eventually left my car in the Kroger parking lot near our home.

And I never got an opportunity to change that paperwork at Corinne's daycare center.

Spotlight on Abuse-Protective Orders:

All states have a law in place to help you obtain a protective/restraining order (the specifics are determined by the state you live in). Protective/restraining orders do not prevent your abuser from harming or stalking you; it is just a piece of paper. In fact, it may increase the likelihood of further violence. HOWEVER, it gives you legal grounds to have them arrested if they break the order.

Orders not only protect the victim, but they can protect current romantic partners of the victim, friends, children, roommates, other family members, and some states allow the pets to be listed. If you share children, orders of protection can make provisions for child support or visitation. Types of protection include:

- **No contact.** The abuser cannot call, email, text, or get anyone else to contact the victim on his behalf.
- **Move out.** The abuser is required to move out of the shared dwelling with the victim for a period of time.
- **Peaceful/non-violent contact**. Communication is limited to the discussions about the care of a child and/or visitation.
- **Firearms.** The abuser cannot purchase a gun, and two-thirds of all states require abusers to surrender all guns.
- **Stay away**: This order prohibits the abuser from coming with 100 yards (state dependent) of the victim, her home, school, church, or car.

- **Counseling:** Orders the abuser to go through counseling or a family violence intervention program (classes about domestic violence) for a minimum of twenty-four weeks. This clause is state dependent ("Orders of Protection," n.d.).

What can you do about it?

Hebrews 11:1 "Now faith is the reality of what is hoped for, the proof of what is not seen."

You can receive an order of protection at your local court house when you present evidence of the abuse. Evidence can consist of text messages, police reports, and/or pictures of any injuries sustained. If you are being stalked or abused, make sure you are documenting EVERYTHING.

You do not have to go through this alone. Contact your local domestic violence shelter or agency for information about the laws in your state. Beloved, even when you feel like you can't put your faith in "the system," know that you can always put your faith in God. He has the power to turn ALL things around for your good so don't give up! Even if you feel like you're not getting help everywhere you turn, continue to pray and continue to seek help until someone helps you.

Pray: Father God teach me how to put my faith in you. I know that you will turn things around for my good because I trust in you and you have called me for a kingdom purpose. You alone are my help. Give me wisdom on who I need to seek and what agencies can help me. You are my light, shield, and protection. Place a hedge of protection around me and my family that is so strong, no harm can come near us. In Jesus's name, Amen.

Chapter 15: Calculated Trapping

Every morning, I woke up feeling more and more hopeless. I didn't know what was going to happen. I just knew I was tired of the things Terrence kept doing.

Tired and scared.

Every morning my alarm played "His Eye on the Sparrow" by Lauryn Hill and Tanya Blount. It gave me the strength to wake up and get my day started. It was my little nudge that let me know God had my back.

As usual, I checked the perimeter of my house from every window before leaving every morning. As I was driving to the daycare, every morning I looked all around for White Chevy Silverados.

I was running late for school so I hurriedly dropped Corinne off by the front door and kissed her bye.

I got back into my car, took a look at my hair in the mirror, and shook my head.

"Girl, you look a hot mess!" I said to myself and started laughing. I put the key in the ignition and turned my car to exit on the right side of the driveway when Terrence's white truck pulled up in front of the exit, blocking my way.

"Shit! What does he want?"

He got out of the truck and slung his camouflage book bag across his back. He walked towards me with his hands in a "stop" gesture. I left the car in "drive" just in case…

Instead of coming to my driver's side window, he went to the passenger side, put the book bag on the ground, and motioned for me to let the window down.

"Hey, Terrence."

"I just want to know if we gon' be together?" he shouted.

"Terrence, I am running late for work. Can we talk this afternoon?" He began to unzip his book bag and reached inside.

"But you don't eva answer that damn phone! How the hell we gon' talk?"

"Can we please just…"

He quickly interrupted me. "I just want to know if we gon' be together!" Something deep inside me said, "No matter what you do, don't tell him 'no.'"

I put the car in park and turned all the way around in my seat to face him. "Terrence Sherod Roberson, I love you so much. Can we please talk about this when I get home this afternoon?"

At that point, he took his hands out of the book bag, zipped it back up, and put his whole head inside the window. His facial expression had softened.

"You promise to call me as soon as you get off?"

"I promise, baby."

Then he pushed his eyebrows together in a puzzled expression and asked, "What the hell is wrong with yo' hair?"

"I told you I was running late for work. I'm going to fix it when I get there." We both started laughing.

He went back to his truck, blew the horn at me, and drove off.

I found out later that day from Jemel, Terrence's boss and friend, that Terrence came to his house after seeing me at the daycare center. He told Jemel that he wanted his family back and everything seemed to be going wrong in his life.

Jemel then said that Terrence reached into his camouflage book bag, handed him a gun, and asked him to hold it for him. It was the same book bag from that morning!

Terrence told him that he was going to get some help and wanted him to keep the gun until he returned to get it. Jemel said he had the intention of giving the gun to Terrence's daddy.

I received a call later that evening from Terrence telling me he had checked into a mental facility to get some help in an effort to win me back (I found out later he would use this hospital stay as a means to get out of the REAL trouble he was about to get us all into).

I had made an appointment to get my hair done that afternoon, but I was unable to go because of what I found out. My hairdresser, Nicole, was concerned when I didn't show up for my appointment and had texted me about my whereabouts.

The next morning, I texted her back.

Me: *Hey Nicole! I'm ok. Terrence threatened to hurt me at school, broke into my home, stole my car, and tried to pull a gun on me at Corinne's daycare. But because of God, he has now checked himself in the mental ward at the VA hospital. Because of all that drama, I had to change my locks and the alarm system so I have no money to see you.*

Nicole: *I love you, Kimya.*

Me: *I love you, too, and I will see you on Thursday. (smiley face emoji)*

Nicole: *I am really worried about you.*

Me: *I know. I'm worried, too. He couldn't handle that I've finally said that I don't want to be with him.*

After only two days, Terrence voluntarily left the hospital and asked if we could get back together. I told him that I was going to file for divorce and would send the papers.

Because I stood my ground about wanting a divorce and not wanting to see Terrence, his phone calls and texts began escalating after checking himself out of the hospital.

At some point, he went back home to Glenwood to be with his family. Since he broke his telephone, he bought a prepaid phone and began alternating between that phone and his parents' phones so he could call and/or text me endlessly.

Dear Reader,

I wanted to share a word for word account of our texts and telephone calls so you can have a true picture of what excessive messaging looks like and to display the cycle of abuse even in the messages: being nice and apologetic and then returning to guilt and threats. It is all about power and control.

Our relationship would change for good after this exchange of messages.

Love,

Kimya

Cell Phone Transcripts

September 8, 2011
Phone rings9:42p
Text received: 9:47p
Terrence: *Hey, Kimya. I was calling about info for payment.*
Me: *The phone payment is $300. Go on and send it in the mail.*

He wanted to show a kind gesture by helping me pay the mortgage. I believe he thought that if he started helping me with the household bills, I would change my mind. The worst thing I could have done was respond to texts and periodically answer the calls. It only reinforced this erratic behavior and caused him to become angrier.

Phone rings	9:42p
	9:52p
	10:05p
	10:08p
	10:10p
	10:16p
Text received:	10:16

Terrence: I was talking about the house payment.
Me: Don't worry about that.
Terrence: Why cant u answer the phone?
Me: I don't want to talk.

Phone rings	10:18p
	10:19p
	10:20p
	10:20p
	10:20p
	10:22p

10:23p

10:24p

10:26p

10:26p

Text received: 10:31p

Terrence: *When can we talk?*

Ok.

Ok.

I won't worry no more. Whatever happens, it will be.

Me: *Thank you.*

Terrence: *I won't worry anymore.*

Me: *Thank you—just send me $300 for your phone.*

Text received:: 10:36 p

Terrence: *I can see now I told u. I will go to the Sprint store and pay that bill. I was only calling u about the house payment.*

Terrence: *I will go to the sprint store and pay.*

Terrence: *I reckon we just talk in court.*

Phone rings: 10:49

Text sent: 10:49

Me: *What now?*

Terrence: *What u can't answer?*

Terrence: *What u can't answer?*

Terrence: *Uhmm*

Terrence: *I said we still need to talk next week, next Month, sometime face to face.*

Terrence: *That all.*

Text received: 10:55p

Terrence: *That is the only way I will sign those papers.*

Terrence: *I will like to pay that house not first, but u insist about the phone. Ur wishes will be granted.*

Terrence: *Why dont u want to talk to me?*
U don't have to.
Why dont u want to talk to me?
Why dont u want to talk to me?
Why dont u want to talk to me?
Why dont u want to talk to me?
Why dont u want to talk to me?
Why dont u want to talk to me?
Why dont u want to talk to me?
Why dont u want to talk to me?
Why dont u want to talk to me?
Hello?

Kim, read this message if u love me. Please. I know I have sent my family through a lot, and I am truly sorry. I won't do it no more because I have a problem with depression and anxiety. Ever since I been diagnose with this disease(sarcoidosis), it has been hard to cope with. When I had u, I was always scared to talk to u, and it is a lot to do with this.

I don't know what happened, but my fear got the best of me, and I am sorry. But Kim, I need u to help me get through this. U always said U would be there for me. I really need u as a friend more than anything. Just want to talk. When u don't answer the telephone, I always think the worse, and then u say u Don't want to be bothered. That hurts because I always have a problem with communication.

When I met u. I thought I was in a different world. U accepted me for that. Yes, I have been going to the doctor. It's working.

It seems every time I try to do something, it is too late, but like u say, it is too late for us, but sometime I wish you would call. I am at my parents' house or call me on my mother's or father's cell phones. I know u are through a lot yourself so I sometime understand, but I wish u would at least call just to say are u alright.

U know it hurt me not to talk to those kids. I have only good intentions, and u don't ever call me again.

U know it hard for me to even talk to my parents. I know u say I have them, but I do cherish them, but I still can't talk to them. It is hard to explain, but I can't and can.

But like I say, if u could find the strength just to call, I promise I wont ask nothing about us just casual conversation. That's all.

U know I haven't slept in my bed since we separated. I always sleep on the floor

Or couch sometime if I need some hope. I really scared on going back to the doc for sarcoidosis. I don't know what he is going to tell me.

Ever since doc told me my life is in jeopardy, I am so scared. I really couldn't tell u, remember? I cried it. It seemed my whole life changed for the worse.

Everybody say u will be alright, but everybody didn't have what I had, and I am sorry for that. I want to hear your voice. if u do decide to text or call, please call before u text. this is my father phone.

September 14, 2011(Phone rings)

12:06 a.m.

12:32 a.m.

1:53 a.m.

1:54 a.m.

2:24 a.m.

I got tired of the endless phone calls, so I finally answered at 3:12 a.m.

"Hello," I answered while straining to open my eyes to see clearly.

"So, you finally decided to pick up the damn phone. What you doing? Fucking somebody?"

"No, Terrence. I was asleep," I answered through staggered yawns. "I have to get up and go to work in the morning. You know that. What's going on?"

"You seeing somebody, Kim?" he snapped.

"No, Terrence. I told you I am not interested in seeing anybody else. I love you, but I just want to focus on my kids and start over."

I wanted him to believe that I still loved him because I was afraid of what he might do to me if I wasn't super nice to him. Maybe he would hit me. Maybe he would try to beat me up.

"Well, I couldn't handle it if you was seeing someone else."

"Terrence, it just didn't work out between us. That doesn't mean that you are bad or I am bad. It just means that we are bad for each other. This is your opportunity to marry someone else and have children with her. Something I couldn't do for you."

"I don't want nobody else. Why don't you give me a chance to show you that. Meet me at Waffle House on Saturday. I will sign them papers if you meet me just one last time."

"I don't trust you Terrence. You might try to hurt me," I replied with hesitation.

"Ain't nobody tryin' to hurt yo ass. Just meet me one last time."

Just to see how he would respond, I sat up in the bed, pulled my comforter up to my chin, and said with a shaky voice, "Well, I am going to bring the sheriff with me...just to make sure."

He chuckled a little bit. "Go ahead an bring 'im with your scary ass. I told you that I am not going to hurt you."

"Well let me pray about it, and I will let you know," I said.

"Ok, go back to sleep. I love you, Kim."

"OK." It was all I could manage to say. Not knowing what to do, I drifted back to sleep, knowing that the alarm would catch me in just a couple of hours. The next sound I heard was the text indication tone. I rolled over and groaned.

I finally looked at the text at 6:08 a.m. on Wednesday, September 14th, just as I was leaving the house.

Terrence: Tell Theron and Corrine I said hello, please. U will get money next week.

Text received: September 15, 2011 6:47a.m.

Terrence: Sorry for callin' u so much. I thought u were ignoring me. Sorry. when we get back together and when it come to signing that teaching contract. u won't have too.

Text received: 7:08 a.m.

Terrence: U can concentrate on getting your mba and baking.

Text received: 7:32a

Terrence: Remember, we will both go to court and we will both be under oath. They are going to ask about our contact. I am not going to lie so u might want to drop the divorce.

Remember, we will both go to court and we will both be under oath. They are going to ask about our contact. I am not going to lie so u might want to drop the divorce.

Text received: 7:35a

Terrence: U going to put the both of us in jeopardy. I ask u not to file this yet. Let us resolve this like adults cause I will never go to court again without a lawyer.

Text received: 7:40a

Terrence: I am asking u to at least do that. Stop being so hasty to do things. I take those vows very serious.

I want to continue to see the both of them children. I love them both. I wasn't lying about the Atlanta film fest and getting T.J. to work some films in atl.

I even seen tyler perry shop in atl

Text received: 7:55a

Terrence: So please stop that divorce paper. I will sign them, and let's try this counseling.

I didn't mean to go off in July, but every time I say let's try it u always back out. and remember as far as ur friends are concerned... misery loves company I wish u would stop talking to them

Text sent 7:57a

Me: Terrence, we are not getting back together. I wish you nothing but blessings from God in your future, BUT we will no longer be married. I'm sorry.

Terrence: Talking to them friends of yours most of them never being married and our troubles are different from theres we need to work it out by ourselves

Text received: 7:59a

Terrence: Okay.

Text received: 8:03a

Terrence: We will see.

Terrence: U heard me.

Terrence: And I wish u will stop being afraid of me.

Terrence: U are supposed to be working.

Terrence: Never say never, never again.

Terrence: Ps don't text anymore I am leaving. Coming back to atlanta

Text received: 10:04a

Terrence: This why I couldnt sleep last night. I knew it was something; I felt it

Terrence: U dont have to answer the phone.

Text received: 10:04a

Terrence: U can't answer the telephone. Just checking on u.

Text received: 10:07p

Terrence: Kim I am scared of this divorce Read: matt 5 And 32 Matt 19 and 19   mark 12 and 25

    Kim I am scared of this divorce Read: matt 5 And 32 Matt 19 and 19   mark 12 and 25

    Kim I am scared of this divorce Read: matt 5 And 32 Matt 19 and 19   mark 12 and 25

    I know you don't see any hope for us, but there is.

    When I went to the hospital to get help, I went just for our marriage that is the only reason. I thought I could win u back and show u I do care about my family.

Terrence: Yes, I was depressed. That's all. Getting divorce who don't be depressed.

I would like to get the kids once a month just to hang out with them

U don't have to worry about what some women think about me or me cheating on you because I am scared of even a relationship with another woman because of what the bible speak of divorce.

Text received: September 16, 2011 @ 12:01 a.m.

Terrence: I am really scared of this divorce thing because the bible don't speak well of it in the New Testament. I am just really scared of divorce. Everything can be work out.

I prayed to God that you will stop being scared of me. I don't feel no harm against my family. That would be crazy of me. I wish u would stop saying that too. I truly luv u.

And with Theron, I just need to spend more time with him, and I will under circumstances if u allow me to spend time with him

Terrence: I know u want me to stop calling, but it hard and I am sorry.

U have to forgive me. I will be leaving atlanta in the morning. I been by my auntie house. She cook so don't worry about calling. I won't be here. Why did u call anyway?

Sorry about today it suppose to be happy but it wasn't. I'm sorry.

Today is our anniversary

It should be happy anniversary.

U don't have to call back mail that key to my parents house

U don't have to call back mail that key to my parents house

Text Sent:

Me: What's the address?

Terrence: I gave it to you look on the court papers.

Terrence: U dont know it.

Terrence: u dont know it

Terrence: u dont know it

Terrence: u dont know it

Terrence: u dont know it

Terrence: u dont know it

U don't have it written down.

U remember everything else. Why cant you remember that Uhhhmmm.

Terrence: Hey, when r u going to mail my key?

Hey when r u going to mail my key

Hey when r u going to mail my key

Hey when r u going to mail my key

Hey when r u going to mail my key

Hey when r u going to mail my key

Hey when r u going to mail my key

Hey when r u going to mail my key

Hey when r u going to mail my key

Hey when r u going to mail my key

Hey when r u going to mail my key

Hey when r u going to mail my key

Hey when r u going to mail my key

Hey when r u going to mail my key

Hey when r u going to mail my key

Hey when r u going to mail my key

Hey when r u going to mail my key
Please text back, and let me know.
U haven't answered the question.
U havent answer the question

Me: Today or tomorrow – what's the address?

Terrence: I gave u the address. U don't have it.

Me: Don't have it anymore. Send the whole address.

Terrence: Ok, dont worry about it cause I think I gave u the wrong address anyway.

Me: Well, that means the sheriff won't be able to find you. I'll call your mother.

Terrence: No she don't know the address I won't be at my parents' house. No way. And I don't know the address. All they are doing is serving some papers; I dont have to be here. Whatever address I gave u. That was it.

Besides, don't talk to my mother. Remember that she wanted to call u to check on u, but u said that y'all dont need to talk.

Me: If you gave me the wrong address the last time, then they will not be able to find it

Terrence: Roberson, baby, everybody knows us.

Me: I'll just call your mom; you play too many games.

Terrence: Okay, I am not playing games. I just don't remember it. Oh well.

No games. I just can't remember. U know the hell with that key and everything else.

I told u I forgot the address, but u said I was playing games as usual. Sorry for ever calling or texting. I will be glad when those papers come

That would be the final text I ever got from Terrence.

Spotlight on Abuse-Stalking: It doesn't feel

good to be stalked by someone. At first, you might be
tempted to think that such behavior is cute. I have even
heard others talking about the behaviors in a very casual
manner like, "Look, he still wants me," or "Man, he is
always blowing up my phone[14]." However, stalking is
SERIOUS business and usually means the person's
behavior is elevated to the point where an explosion is
going to occur. It is not a matter of "if" an explosion will
occur; it is a matter of "when.".

Stalking is a pattern of behaviors that include receiving
undesired attention, contact, and harassment from another
person, causing you to feel increasingly fearful. Behaviors
include but are not limited to:

- **Pop- ups.** Memorizing your schedule and coming
  to places you go.
- **Unwanted attention.** Repeated phone calls,
  texts, emails, and/or letters as well as sending
  unwanted gifts.
- **Cyber abuse.** Contacting you or posting about
  you on social media and creating websites and/or
  fake profile pages with your picture on them
- **Theft.** Stealing things that belong to you.
- **Threats**. Making threats against your family or
  friends ("Stalking," 2015).

---

[14] calling repeatedly

What can you do about it?

1 Peter 5:8 Be alert! Be serious! Your adversary the Devil is prowling around like a roaring lion, looking for anyone he can devour

If you are being stalked, I cannot reiterate enough that you should have a "no contact" rule. Keep all messages, texts, and social media posts for your records. Also, let someone close to you know what is going on and send them the messages, too. You can do this by taking screenshots and emailing them to trusted friends and family members.

Keep a journal of all interactions with him. Of course you can take out an order of protection so when the stalker violates it, you can have him arrested. As always, create a safety plan with a domestic violence advocate and consider joining a support group or try counseling to help you deal with the emotional roller coaster you are experiencing.

Continue to pray and seek godly counsel. Your Father in Heaven cares all about the things that are concerning you and wants you to be safe. Don't lose hope. Remember, if God be for you, who DARES to stand against you!

Pray: Father God, I know that my adversary is walking about like a roaring lion seeking whom he can devour. Help me to put my trust in your ability to save and protect me. Fill me with hope for the future. Let me know that you shall never leave or forsake me. Give me security in the love you have for me. Strengthen me to see this battle through until the end. Help me to be victorious. In Jesus's name, Amen.

Chapter 16: Here Lies Kimya Roberson

In the drizzly, early hours of September 20, 2011, I found myself on my typical route down Highway 138 from Conyers to Stockbridge to drop Corinne off at daycare so she could catch the school bus to Lorraine Elementary; I was late as usual. I could never quite leave the house on time, but today I was much later than was customary.

I drove my 2006 gray Toyota Camry around the curves of that blackened highway as if I were on auto-pilot. Driving sixty-five MPH in a 55 zone went against how I would normally drive, but I was determined that I would make it to school on time that day.

Despite the nagging feeling that I should slow down because the roads were indeed slippery from the rain, I sped along the road with only minutes to spare. All types of thoughts raced through my mind.

"Okay, Kimya, let's get it," I muttered under my breath.

"What you say, Mommy?" asked Corinne.

"Nothing, baby."

"Don't you think you're going pretty fast, Mommy?"

"Girl, you got that shoe on your foot yet? Don't worry about me."

Corinne came out of our house that morning with one shoe on and one shoe off..

If I dropped her off at 6:30, I would only have twenty minutes to get to work and that was totally unacceptable because it was easily a thirty-minute ride back to my school from daycare center.

So, I pushed the pedal a little closer to the floor...sixty-five mph...seventy mph...and then back to fifty-five mph.

"Ohhh, I don't want or need a ticket." I began to slow down to go the speed limit again.

As I signaled to turn right onto 155, something struck me. I forgot to say my daily prayer affirmations that usually begin my morning.

"Father God, send forth all your warring angels to force out, cast out, and keep out all demonic spirits. Don't allow them to attach themselves to us, manifest in front of us, or torment or torture us in any way, shape, form or fashion. In the name of Jesus, Amen."

Corinne repeated, "Amen."

I had just a quarter of a mile to the driveway. I didn't realize what was waiting up ahead for me.

I pulled up into the half-moon-shaped driveway under the awning so we wouldn't get wet.

If I had been paying close attention, I would have known it was him.

Ever since the previous daycare incident, I had been so careful...until that day.

I was always careful to check the perimeter of my house before leaving for work daily, scan the parking lot at school for white Chevy Silverados, and I would even have my next-door neighbor, Patrice, check my house for his vehicle before I came home. Mostly because Kelly told me that I needed to do that. Not because I thought he would become as desperate as he was that day.

I didn't look. I was late and distracted.

I was so distracted that I didn't look closely at the White Saturn S.U.V driving back and forth repeatedly on the main road. I just assumed that because it was raining, it must have been another parent waiting for me to leave my position under the awning so that he/she could park there.

I quickly dismissed any other thoughts when I looked at the clock on my dashboard and realized it was 6:25.

"Oh crap! Corinne, do you have your shoes on?" I snapped at her.

"No," she replied hesitantly.

Getting out of the car, I walked around to the back-passenger side door where she was seated and angrily pulled it open. At the same time, he pulled up alongside my car in my blind spot to the left of me, camouflaging his vehicle in the shadows of the morning and acting as if he were any other parent dropping off his child.

"Cora Jean Elizabeth, I need you to take yourself over to that ramp and put your shoes on right now! I am already late," I barked.

"Mommy, I will put my shoe on, but I need you to sign my papers for school, too," she replied as she sheepishly smiled at me and slid on her bottom across the seat to exit through the door. She went to sit down on the ramp like I told her.

I reached in the car to get something, and I closed the door behind her, rolled my eyes towards Heaven, said a prayer that I wouldn't give Corinne a serious tongue lashing, and took a deep breath to calm myself down.

Terrence exited his vehicle, walked with quickened footsteps, rounded the backside of my car, and startled me with a silver, .38 caliber pistol pointed at the side of my face.

"I told you I was going to kill your ass didn't I?" he said and pulled the trigger.

Simultaneously, I heard another voice say very softly, "Turn your head."

"Huh," I thought. The voice sounded like my cousin Jamie, but that was impossible because he died three years earlier.

I turned my head to the left in the direction of the voice, and there wasn't anyone there.

The bullet seared through my right cheek, exited the left side of my face, and went through my car door.

The smell of the gunpowder and sulfur filled my nostrils and mouth with the unmistakable acrid, bitter taste of rotten eggs.

I placed both of my hands on my face in disbelief. When I brought my hands down, they were covered in blood. Watching the crimson drip between my fingers and down to the ground sent my heart racing at speeds only useful for racehorses and track runners.

And he watched me.

I wanted to run but to where?

I saw the playground to the left in the distance, and I thought I could run there to get away from him.

I couldn't.

The next bullet hit me in the left side of the neck. I immediately grabbed the spot and thought of Jamie. Oh no. *Lord, am I going to die?* Jamie was stabbed in the neck, and he died. I was just shot there.

Was that Jamie's voice I heard trying to warn me?

I was trapped.

I began to scream the name of Jesus as I was running in a circle. I was hearing shots ring out like the Fourth of July. I tripped and fell to the ground. More shots.

A million thoughts flooded my brain. Where was Corinne? I didn't see her anywhere. Oh, my gosh! What was my baby thinking?

Terrence stood over me like he stood over those hogs that winter day in Glenwood when he and his daddy castrated all their male hogs.

Again, I heard the voice: "Turn your head." I kept thinking about Jamie.

I began to fight the asphalt with both hands as I frantically turned my head from side to side and shouted, "No, no, no!".

Boom! Another shot hit me in the back of the head, just inches from my left ear.

I stopped screaming, just lay there, and thought: *Jesus help me. Where's my baby?*

Lying in a pool of my own blood, I slowly turned my head to the right. I saw her. Her head dropped. I thought she didn't want to see what was happening to me.

More shots.

I couldn't move. I couldn't scream out. I closed my eyes as he walked back towards me.

Bang. One last shot was fired and hit me in the back. He then got into the White Saturn and drove off.

In the smoke-filled haze of the aftermath of the gunfire, I crawled hastily to my knees and up to my feet. I ran to Corinne's side as she sat looking fearfully from the ramp.

"Look baby, Mommy's al...right..."

There was a gaping hole in the top left corner of her head and blood was pouring from it.

"Oh my God! Corinne, Corinne!"

I could no longer think of my injuries. All I could do was think about her and Theron. I could not die. I had to save my children.

I picked her up, walked up the ramp, kissed her, and sat her down outside the doorway of the daycare center.

I walked in and began shouting. "Help me! Help! Please, we've been shot!" Tears began streaming down my face as I realized that no one from inside the daycare would answer.

Do they hear me?

Do they think he's still here?

I put my face down by the opening and shouted again, "Someone help us, please! We've been shot!"

Well, I knew that we were not going to die like dogs in the street, so I picked up the keypad and began to bang it against the Plexiglas window.

I placed the keypad down and tried desperately to remember the set of codes needed to unlock the door. They had been given to us just weeks before. I always had to pull the little cards out of my purse in order to gain access.

How was I going to get some help for my baby?

I needed to get her off that ramp and into safety.

Then it happened...

Somehow, miraculously, I was able to put in the two sets of codes that gained us entry! I thought Corinne could not walk, but much to my surprise, she got up from the ramp, walked into the lobby area behind me and closed the door.

Upon entering the facility, I overheard Teresa, one of the workers from the early morning shift, talking on the phone with the 911 emergency operator. When she saw Corinne and me, her face turned as white as a ghost as she gasped at us in horror.

At this point, the conversation turned.

The 911 dispatcher gave her instructions on how to handle our injuries and wanted her to remain on the line. We sat down in the waiting area of the center near the front desk. Teresa handed the phone to Emma, another caregiver in the daycare center, and kind of stood in front of us in shock for what seemed like an eternity.

I immediately pulled my baby into my lap and whispered in her ear how much I loved her. I rubbed her back and told her how much Jesus loved her, too. I told her to call on the name of Jehovah.

I sat her down in the chair next to me, placed her face in my hands, and gazed deeply in her eyes.

"Corinne, I am so, so sorry. I am so sorry this happened to you."

She didn't say anything. I kept trying to wipe the blood out of her eyes as it continuously poured.

"Corinne, Mommy loves you so much. Do you understand me, baby?"

Still nothing. She didn't nod her head or speak.

Hot tears began to flood my eyes and pour down my face. I didn't want to lose my baby. I pulled her close to me and began to rock her.

Emma, the older of the two women, told Teresa to move us into another room because children would be coming in and would see us.

I rose from my chair, and we walked into the adjacent room. Corinne sat down on the floor, and I sat in the chair. At this point, the pain was beginning to intensify, and I shook my legs erratically in hopes that it would take the pain and fear away. I held my head closest to my right shoulder because holding it straight up proved to be more of a challenge.

Fortunately, the sheriff arrived and walked into the facility at that time and told me that he was there to help us.

As I turned to look at Corinne, she began to vomit blood all over her shirt. I jumped down onto the floor to try to help her, but I couldn't do anything at all, but hold her and rock back and forth.

I felt so completely helpless.

I looked at the blood-stained footsteps across the white tiled floor of the toddler room and rocked her some more. All I could hear was the rapid tap, tap of Ms. Theresa's footsteps pacing back and forth across the floor and her voice speaking to the nurse on the phone. "Yes, ma'am. Where should I apply the towel?"

I sat glued to that floor, watching in horror as the blood poured down the side of my daughter's face and soaked the blue Supergirl shirt she was wearing...that Supergirl shirt she had practically begged me to buy for her a week ago. She tried in vain to wipe the blood off her face between lapses in consciousness, but it kept running.

At that point, Sheriff Jones sat on the other side of her, and Theresa kept wiping her face with that once white towel. I got back up into my chair.

The scene was surreal. I looked all around that room and saw nothing but little tables with little chairs and colorful walls filled with drawings and paintings created by happy children. But my child wasn't happy...not today...

"Oh Lord, please. Not my child, not my baby," I whispered repeatedly under my breath.

All she wanted to do was go to school this morning. All she wanted to do was to catch the bus to her school. She had nothing to do with this.

Why would he do this to her?

How could I let this happen?

I just wanted to start over and have a second, no third, chance to finally be happy...to have the family I always desired.

I was tired of the abuse, tired of the tears, tired of me being so desperate that I settled for anything and everything in the name of love. And now, tired of the pain. I was growing faint from the pain.

Trying to deal with the excruciating pain I was in, I shook my left leg as hard as I could, thinking it would take my mind off the pain...pain that seared through my body like an earthquake registering a 10 on the Richter scale. I watched streams of blood pour down my white school shirt and dot my khaki pants that I planned to wear to work.

I tried to change positions in the chair in order to deal with the pain. Shifting back and forth in that chair, I unsure of what to do. Finding a comfortable position in the chair would prove to be impossible.

Watching her drift in and out of consciousness was more than I could take. I jumped onto the juice-stained, ABC rug and shook her shoeless foot.

"Corinne! Corinne! Wake up! Baby, I love you."

Her eyes flickered opened for a second, and she caught a glimpse of me.

Sheriff Jones demanded, "Don't do that to her. You need to do something productive. That is not helping anyone, especially not her."

In an effort to distract me, he pointed sternly in the direction of the chair. "Get back into that seat and read the sign on the wall."

I stared at that Days of the Week poster. "I don't want to read any damned sign!" I shouted.

I looked at my precious baby lying on the white, cold, tiled floor. Blood poured down her freshly-braided cornrows, and her eyes rolled in the back of her head. She vomited oceans of green bile on her blue Super Girl shirt. These images sent feelings of devastation through me.

Sheriff Jones rubbed her arms and gently called her name. "Corinne...Corinne...sweetie...stay with me..." He tried to keep her awake.

I reluctantly slid back into that yellow toddler chair. I didn't know what to do about her...me...anything.

On top of that, all I felt was pain. I tried holding my head over to my right side. Every beat of my heart sent a gush of blood and pain to the left side of my neck, forming a clot from the bullet jammed there. This made it increasingly hard to straighten my head or speak.

I started breathing erratically.

The hole from the bullet that pierced the side of my face produced a salty river of thick, warm liquid in my mouth that I couldn't swallow or spit out. All I could do is let it run. My mouth no longer worked.

The pain...

The memory of what happened just five minutes ago...

My baby...would she live or die?

So many thoughts sped through my mind like an out of control locomotive...

I felt so helpless.

I tried talking to her, but she could no longer respond to me.

Did she know I loved her more than anything?

Did she know she was my sunshine?

Did she know she didn't deserve this?

My tears washed all the blood out of my face and onto my white shirt that was already darkened from my other wounds. I was sobbing uncontrollably now.

I began rocking in the chair to try to deal with the excruciating pain, but all I could do was think about her and my son, Theron.

Oh God! He was at home all alone!

What was going to happen to my son?

If that monster could do this to her, what would he do to my son?

Oh my God!

Waves of devastating pain now possessed my body as I shook in complete heartbreak.

All I could do was pray out loud and repeat over and over again: "Holy Spirit...please don't let him take my baby from me. Please don't let him take my baby. Not the baby."

It took about twenty minutes for the first ambulance to arrive, and they tried to take me first.

"No!" I shouted in protest, "I don't want to go. Please take my baby."

"Ma'am, we have some help here for her, too."

The paramedics motioned for me to sit on the gurney. Once I did, they strapped me down.

I didn't get an opportunity to kiss my baby or tell her goodbye.

I just continued to pray, and strangely enough, when they pushed me outside and into the ambulance, a strong peace came over me.

Part II: Rehab and Rebirth

Dear Reader,

Part two of the book begins when I left the hospital. I asked my social media audience what they wanted while I wrote the book. Overwhelmingly, they said they wanted diary entries; therefore, most of the pages are the exact notes that I wrote directly to God about what I was thinking, feeling, and experiencing at that time.

Love,

Kimya

2 Corinthians 5:17 *"Therefore, if anyone is in Christ, he is a new creation; old things have passed away, and look, new things (a)have come.*

"

Chapter 17: Guilty as Charged

September 27, 2011

I left the medical center exactly one week after the shooting. It was just as much a shock to me as it was to anyone else. The nurses proclaimed that I would be in the hospital for months, and I promised that I would be out of the hospital by the end of the week because I had to get to my baby.

Sandy and Kelly came to pick me up that day, and even though I was ordered to go straight home to begin taking a plethora of medicine, you already know where my first stop was on the way.

We pulled into the parking garage of Egleston hospital and parked near the elevator. I needed someone to help me walk short distances because I was on so much medication; I felt dizzy most of the time.

Upon exiting the elevator on the floor where the Intensive Care Unit (ICU) was located, I was immediately escorted into the family waiting area and was greeted by the Williams clan. It felt so comforting to see all of them there.

Margaret, Corinne's grandmother, introduced me to one of the nurses on staff at the front desk. Even she had encouraging words for me. She came from around her desk to give me a hug.

After I was given my official purple "parent" badge, Margaret escorted me to the set of double doors where the intercom to the ICU staff would buzz me in to see my princess.

Corinne's nurse, Abby, was there and introduced herself to me. She was a short woman with blonde hair that was as bright as her personality. She had it pulled back into the most elegant French roll and wore small, black-rimmed glasses prominently on her soft, brown eyes. To top it all off, she had on pumpkin scrubs as October was only days away. Abby looked so friendly and acted as though she genuinely cared about Corinne and me.

Abby complimented me on how well I looked and immediately gave me a hug. She told me that Corinne was a fighter and was doing much better than expected.

We stopped at the huge sink in the entrance to the ICU to scrub my hands before entering her room. I was so anxious to see her. My heart began beating in my chest because I didn't know what I was going to find when I saw my little girl. It seemed to be an extremely long walk to the room where she lay waiting me.

On the way, Abby introduced me to everyone in the unit that was responsible for Corinne's care or who had taken a personal interest in her. Many of them took their time to greet me with a hug or handshake. They were all full of encouraging words about our incident and that helped me feel a bit stronger.

Outside her room, the glass doors housed a picture of Corinne that we had taken at Christmas last year. She looked so beautiful in that picture. She had on a deep scarlet dress made of crushed velvet. Looking at her beautiful smile on that picture, made me remember happier times. I could only imagine what I was about to see.

I looked through the glass into her room while Abby continued to talk to me. There were at least a dozen helium balloons on her dresser with various messages of encouragement—"Get Well Soon," "I Love You," etc. There were huge helium-filled animal figures as well. It seemed as if she had tons of stuffed animals lying on her bed, desk, chair, and dresser as well. Corinne had everything that would have made any sick child feel better, but she didn't even know they existed.

Abby continued talking to me about something, but I really didn't hear anything she said as my thoughts took over. All I could remember was that gun pointed in my face. All I could see was blood pouring from Corinne's head and her vomiting bile and falling in and out of consciousness. I blinked my eyes a couple of times to blot out the tears that were beginning to stream down my face.

"Are you ready to go in, sweetie?" Abby inquired.

"Yes," came out of my mouth, but my feet were full of lead.

Nothing could have prepared me for what I saw when I entered Corinne's room. I don't even remember who entered that room with me. I don't remember where anyone was. It was as if I were in some alternative world.

My baby girl was lying in the bed with one eye closed and one eye partially open. An elongated plastic tube was pushed deep down into her mouth to help her to breathe. She had a slender tube pushed down into her half-shaven skull that regulated her brain fluids, and she had another thin tube in her nose leading to her stomach that fed her. There were blood pressure monitors, IVs, and all types of machines that went blink, whir, and zip around her.

Corinne was in a coma.

My legs felt weak and wobbly. I needed help to steady myself.

Tears began streaming out of my eyes as I leaned over her and began rubbing her arms and legs.

"Hey baby."

No response.

I sang to her the words to "You are my Sunshine" as I had done so many times before.

I choked on the words like something painful was coming out of my mouth.

More tears. Oh God. It hurt so badly. What did he do to my baby?

"I really began to cry when I sang the part about not taking my sunshine away."

I was careful not to let my tears touch her face as I kissed her repeatedly on her cheeks and whispered in her ear.

"Hi, beautiful. Mommy is here to see you. I love you, and I am ready for you to come home. Now you are going to have to work hard to get out of here. I miss you. T.J. misses you, and Peanut misses you. All day long Peanut walks in and out of your room, sniffing your bed, and wagging his tail, looking for you. When I walk downstairs, he lies on his belly by the door waiting for you to come home from school. So, little lady, I want you to do what you have to do to get home. I love you, okay?"

There was no response. But I knew she could hear me.

Margaret led me out of the room. Right outside the door, I fell to the floor on my knees and wept uncontrollably. She didn't look so good!

"Oh my God! This is all my fault. This is all my fault."

Margaret helped me off the floor and hugged me.

"No, no...She looks so much better than she did. She is doing so much better. Don't worry."

"She does?" I asked and wiped the tears from my face on the back of my sleeve.

"Yes, every day the swelling around her face goes down, and they remove at least one tube daily. They were saying that she would be here for months, but the doctors are amazed at her recovery and are saying that her stay may be shorter than they thought."

"Ok" was all I could seem to mutter. I was so overcome with grief.

All I could see was my child suffering in that bed.

All I could see was him shooting her.

All I could see was that it was my fault.

I was anxious to speak with a doctor, but there were none available.

"Look, sweetie, her bed is large enough for you to lie down in when you come to visit. You can lay right next to your little girl and talk to her when you come," Abby said to me as she came around the corner and heard Margaret talking to me.

I was pleased at that prospect. I was on at least seven different medications that left me feeling either dizzy or drowsy. I could only come for about an hour to see her daily because without the medication, the pain from my jaw, neck, and back would surge through my body, leaving me feeling such intense pain that I couldn't stand it.

I cried on my way out of the hospital and all the way home. I feel like I failed my little girl.

Chapter 18: Adjusting to a New Life

October 2011

On Sunday, I was quite surprised when I opened Facebook to see the many well wishes from strangers, friends, and family.

"How did they all know about this?" I asked Michael.

"Girl, it's been all over the news!"

I was shocked and afraid of this at the same time. I began thinking. *Why would this be all over the news? Am I in trouble?*

He told me that people from all over the city were encouraged by my story and wanted to support us.

Posted on Facebook by me on October 2, 2011

I want to thank you all for all your prayers and words of encouragement. When I look on this page and see all of your prayers, it makes me feel so good knowing that you care.

Thank you for letting God use you in such an awesome way to minister to me. Please keep praying until my daughter WALKS out of that hospital totally healed and delivered by God.
Kimya

Michael and I only went out on four dates before the shooting, and when I woke up from my coma, he was there. I never imagined a man could love me as much as he did.

He drove trucks for a living and came from South Carolina to visit me on the weekends. When he left Sunday night, I couldn't sleep.

Lying in my bed at 1 a.m., 2 a.m., and 3 a.m., and I still couldn't sleep. I rolled over to Michael's side of my bed and started smelling the pillow in hopes of catching a hint of his cologne. Sniff. Sniff—no luck. I could only seem to sleep when he was present. I felt safe with him next to me. He gave me so much peace. I wrote this in my diary...

Diary Entry Monday, October 3, 2011

For the first time since the shooting, I am alone in my house.

I know that Terrence is in jail, but fear and anxiety have taken over. Every sound, crack, voice, and truck rolling down the street makes my heart beat a little faster, and sometimes I cannot stop the tears from falling.

Michael had to get back on the road to go to work. Being a truck driver took him away from me for five days, but I just wait in anticipation for him to get back to me. Tonight, is going to prove to be hard. All I wanted to do was pick up the phone, call Michael, and tell him to come back to my house.

Since he was not there, calling his phone was the next best thing. He was on the road and hearing his voice would lull me back into sound sleeping.

"Hey Michael."

"Hey, babe. Whatcha' doin' up this time 'a night?'"

"Michael, I can't go to sleep. I keep thinking someone is out there. What if his mom and dad are mad at me and want to get back at me? What if he breaks out of jail? He's right around the corner from me, you know? Every time I try to sleep, I keep seeing the shooting over and over. I don't know what to do. I miss you so much cuz the only way I can sleep is if you're holding me."

"I know babe. That's when you open your mouth, snore, and spit comes outcho' mouth all over my chest," he said and laughed loudly.

I started laughing, too. He could always crack a joke or something to get my mind off of what was really hurting me. He always had that effect on me. I loved that about him.

"I do not snore or drool, Michael Langley!" We laughed and talked until I fell asleep with the phone cradled under my ear...and I slept all night.

Diary Entry Tuesday, October 4, 2011

Dear Father,

Today Corinne is going to rehab. I know I am not supposed to go, but I AM going! I called Gretchen (one of my former coworkers and good friends) *and got her to take me to Egleston.*

Just two weeks after the shooting, Corinne was being transported to Scottish Rite by ambulance. The nurse told me that she would learn how to walk and talk again there. I was so excited to hear that! Just two weeks prior, that didn't even seem possible.

Diary entry Thursday, October 6, 2011

Dear Father,

I'm waiting here for Rayna to come and pick me up to take me to Scottish Rite to see Corinne. She and her husband, Miguel, came to see Corinne and they brought one of those digital picture frames with pictures of all of us and Peanut for Corinne. She loved it! Even when we can't be there, she can see us. When she saw a picture of Peanut, she began to cry. Although it hurt me to see her cry about him, it made me feel good to see some emotion come from her. She hasn't cried, smiled or anything since the shooting.

I have an appointment with someone on her team today. Yesterday, I heard her say, "Zoe." I was so excited! That is her doll's name.

Rayna and I were in Corinne's room when the speech language pathologist brought her into the room.

"Corinne, who are these ladies in your room?"
Corinne looked very puzzled and paused for a long time.

"Uhh."

"Baby," I said. "This is Auntie Rayna." I said it very slowly and deliberately, and she repeated what I said.

The nurse then said, "And who is this?"

"Uhh...Auntie...Auntie...Kim," she answered with a puzzled look on her face. .Oh my God! She called me Auntie Kim. My heart sank to the pit of my stomach. Tears were fighting to burst through my lids, but I wouldn't allow that to happen.

"Corinne, baby, I'm...."

The speech language therapist held up her hand to interrupt and told me that Corinne knew who I was; she just didn't have the vocabulary to pull from.

"Give her two choices...kind of like a word bank to pull from." She smiled and nodded for me to continue...

"Corinne. Am I Auntie Kim or am I Mommy?"

Corinne took a deep breath and smiled.

"Mommy."

What a relief.

The Speech Language Pathologist allowed me to tag along with Corinne to do some other activities. Corinne did well reading small phrases and picking up objects that matched the small phrases. She was unable to say the objects in some cases.

I left around 1:30 so that I could get some rest. I had already been at the hospital too long. Technically, I was only supposed to be out of the house for an hour a day. Well, it took an hour to get to Scottish Rite from Covington and an hour back. Nothing was going to keep me from being with my baby.

Nothing.

Rayna and Miguel took me to eat at Piccadilly. It had become my new favorite restaurant because of the soft foods—green beans, chopped beef, and carrot soufflé.

It was getting increasingly difficult to chew and swallow. It seemed like with each passing day, my mouth was getting stiffer and stiffer, and I was unsure why.

Out of the corner of my eye, dressed in a neatly-ironed, red shirt and khaki pants, I saw the mom of one of the students in my class. She cried, hugged me, and paid for my food. She told me that she heard all about what happened to me on the news and assured me that if there were anything I needed, she would help. She gave me her telephone number.

I felt so loved.

Then I came home and slept a while. Rayna and Miguel stayed with me while I slept so they could clean and organize my kitchen. I wrote this in my diary...

Diary entry Friday, October 7, 2011

Dear Lord,

Thank you so much for waking me up this morning. Thank you for my life and my daughter's life. I can never say thank you enough, and I apologize for taking life for granted. Thank you for your many blessings, including support from family and friends and monetary donations; there's just so much to be thankful for.

Yesterday, Corinne didn't know what to call me. That hurt my feelings.

I DID get a little weepy today. I get a little weepy every day when I think about not being able to be at rehab with Corinne. I still feel like it is my fault that she was shot.

I should be there with her every day.

Me.

Not her grandparents.

Me.

I feel guilty about everything.

Thank you God for the strength to do what I can.

Love,

Kimya

Diary Entry October 13, 2011

Much to my surprise, a lady named Deb Lucas created a page on Facebook called "Prayers for Kimya and Corinne." I am really touched by the outpouring of love and encouragement from everyone I know and complete strangers.

I went to see Dr. Henderson for a follow-up visit three weeks after the surgery. He was so impressed with how well I was healing. I kept replaying the conversation in my head that night.

"Wow! You really look good. You're healing up just fine."

"Thank you, Dr. Henderson, but I do have one problem."

"What's that?"

"Every day, it is harder and harder for me to eat. My mouth is not opening as wide as it once did. I don't know what's wrong."

"Smile for me."

I did, and immediately the expression changed on Dr. Henderson's face. He gave me a sealed letter and an appointment with Dr. Dillon, an oral surgeon. I was a little scared about what he told me. I posted this on Facebook...

Facebook post by me

Thank you for your continued prayers. Corinne is improving a little every day. She sat up unsupported for the first time on Friday. When, just a week ago, her body was like a newborn's—unable to support her own weight.

I discovered on Tuesday that I will have to have my mouth wired shut tomorrow for two months because my jaw is broken in two places.

So please continue to pray for my daughter's FULL recovery, my son's emotional state, and for my surgery tomorrow.

May God continue to bless each of you for giving of yourselves in prayer for my family.

Diary entry Friday, October 14, 2011

Dear Father,

Last night, it was very hard for me to sleep. I kept waking up with anxiety about my pending surgery today. I don't really know what to expect, but I'm frightened. I am also mad. I don't know why the doctors didn't catch that the bone in my jaw was broken. Everyone keeps asking me if I am going to sue. I am mad as hell, but I am not going to sue. For what? This man saved my life.

Dr. Dillon said my jaw was fractured like an eggshell and the slightest bump would have meant...I don't even want to think of what it meant. He said that he may have to cut my face to get to my jaw.

Really Lord?!

After healing from being shot in the face, you mean that my face might have to be cut? I don't want to be cut.

It might never heal.

Will I be ugly?

Terrence is going to win if that happens.

I remember the moment when he threatened me about my face. I began replaying that conversation in my mind.

"Yo ass forgets everything. You can't remember your ass from your face!"

Well, because I was starting to feel stronger, I retaliated in my own little way.

"But, I'm still pretty," I said, puckered up my lips like a duck, and rolled my eyes.

He slowly walked to position his body so he was looking straight at me. He touched my face lovingly and asked, "You must think nothin' could happen to that pretty face of yours?"

"No," I said firmly and pulled away from him while being very terrified about what he meant by that. That was probably why he decided to shoot me in the face first. And I didn't want him to be right. He couldn't be right.

Diary entry continued:

I will have four to six weeks or six to eight weeks to wear wires in my mouth.

My body, mind, and spirit feel like they are overloaded. I don't know how to heal when so much is happening to cause me to feel such extreme stress.

Additionally, I am missing my mom terribly. If Mommy were here, she would take care of me and never leave my side. Why do I always feel like I am alone?

My sister Sandy and niece Courtney are here to help me. Sandy is cleaning the house, dodging reporters for me, and making sure we are fed, and taking care of T.J., but I really miss my mom. All I do is cry and sleep. I curl up in a ball and wish that Michael were here with me. I want somebody to hold me, and there is no one.

Diary entry Sunday, October 16, 2011:
Dear God,

Quite a bit has happened over this past week. I've seen my daughter walk for short distances with the aid of a gait belt.

One day I saw her walk up four steps, and then today I saw her walk up one whole flight of steps.

Bailey, my former coworker turned friend, took me to Scottish Rite for my visit today. When we arrived, one of Corinne's nurses told me that she would be practicing walking up the steps today. I was excited and scared at the same time.

Corinne walked up four steps with the nurse holding her gait belt behind her. Upon coming down, we walked down the hall for a bit. My eyes started burning with tears that I wouldn't let fall.

I was so proud of her.

If I had listened to everything those doctors were telling me, I would've been so discouraged.

*Thank you Lord for listening to my prayers.
You are so awesome and worthy to be praised.*

*I didn't know the best surprise of the day was
yet to come.*

*"Do you want to hold her and let her practice
four more steps?" the nurse asked.*

*"Oh yes!" I answered before I knew what I was getting
into.*

*The nurse explained that I would have to show
that I could help guide Corinne with the belt before
the doctors would release her to my care.*

*"Ok, Corinne, we are going to walk up four
more steps," her nurse explained.*

"All!" Corinne exclaimed.

*Before the nurse could protest, my
stubborn daughter began her ascension up the
steps with me in tow. She reached the top of the
first set, sat down completely winded, and
whispered "tired" with a look of pure
exhaustion and satisfaction on her face.*

I smiled in pure admiration.

God, you are so awesome!

I finished my diary entry and began to try to
mentally prepare for my impending surgery the next day.

Michael and I arrived at Gwinnett Medical Center in
Lawrenceville to have my mouth wired shut. I was very
worried about the procedure, but knowing that he would be
by my side made me feel at ease.

Waking up after the surgery and having him right there next to me was so comforting. I couldn't talk at all, and my face was so swollen that I began to cry upon seeing my face.

"Michael," I tried to speak, but I couldn't.

He handed me a pad of paper and pen that the nurse provided for me.

"Were you sleeping?" I wrote. I felt so groggy from the surgery.

"No, babe. I'm sitting right here waiting for you to wake up. You need something?

"Gimme a mirror"

"You sho' you wanna do that?" He slowly handed me the mirror.

"Michael, what's wrong with my face?" I gasped in horror at what I saw. My lips were HUGE and purple. My whole face was at least three times its normal size!

I dropped the mirror, placed my face in my hands, and started crying. "Michael, I am so ugly. My face is so big! What's wrong with me?" I wrote furiously.

"Babe, you aren't ugly. You actually could pass for Jay-Z's sister. Look at the size of those lips. White people actually pay for lips like those."

I stopped crying. "What did you say?" I wrote and began to chuckle.

As usual, he made me laugh because he brought up the fact that I could record a song like Kanye West's "Through the Wire" while looking like Jay-Z's sister or something like that. He said we'd make a lot of money.

His jokes worked for a while until they brought me my dinner: cream of mushroom soup, Jell-O, fruit juice, and Sprite. I started crying again. That stuff looked disgusting and tasted worse

Diary entry Tuesday, October 18, 2011:

My surgery was a success, and I am most thankful that they didn't have to cut my face. Thank you, Father.

Diary entry Wednesday, October 18, 2011

Lord, I don't want this shit!!! How long will I have to eat like this? Even maneuvering the straw in my mouth is a difficult task. I guess I should say, Lucky for me that I have a number of teeth missing which produced a huge hole on the right side of my mouth leading straight through to the left side of my mouth where I was shot. That makes drinking this stuff easier.

No one else came to visit, but it was okay. Nichelle, Tamra (Nichelle's friend), and Pedro (Nichelle's husband) were busy at the house, making everything okay for my return home. Nichelle and Tamra were cleaning and washing our clothes. Pedro was repairing the huge holes in the wall and painting. I couldn't wait to get home and see the finished product.

Diary Entry Thursday, October 20, 2011

Dear Lord,

It is amazing how when things first happened, there was a plethora of people trying to help the family and me. Now that we are one month into this, it is hard to find one person to help out.

A few people check in on us, but I don't have nearly the help I need. That is hard for me to accept, and it hurts deeply. I just have to accept that You are trying to move me to more independence.

Today is a wonderful day, and I am so blessed to be living to see this day! I got Kiki, (the children's cousin and my friend) to pick me up to see Corinne, AND I've had two real days of rest. Best of all, no more nausea, vomiting, or diarrhea!!! Dr. Dillon said that if I ever threw up, I could asphyxiate on my vomit. We had a few close calls, didn't we, Lord? Well, I found out that protein-based milk products are not my friend. Even with that, it was nothing that a little suppository couldn't help.

Much to everyone's surprise, I have learned to speak through these wires. I don't have to write things down anymore!

Well, I guess I **can** *sing a song or something like Kanye or become a ventriloquist like Mike suggested, LOL!*

On top of that, my baby is coming home on Tuesday because they say there is nothing medically wrong with her. She is walking, talking, eating, and almost back to the Corinne she was before the shooting.

I love you, Jehovah God and my Lord and Savior Jesus Christ. I am very thankful and proud that the Holy Spirit heard my cries for help, and You loved me enough to save Corinne and me.

Happy one month anniversary of the shooting.

Thank you for the revelation about my mortgage, too! My house went into foreclosure on September 30th, but because of the outpouring of financial support, all three months have been paid! You are the greatest. I can't wait to see where You lead me to next. It seems that I was reborn on September 20, 2011.

What the devil meant for evil, Jehovah, you have definitely turned around for my good in the name of Jesus! Hallelujah!

I have a wonderful relationship with you; Michael is the love of my life, my children are alive and well, and we are going to build the best relationship. Sandy and Courtney are here with me, Daddy is getting the care he needs, you are providing wealth untold, and for once I feel alive.

Thank you! Thank you!

Friday, October 21, 2011

Dear Lord,

Today these wires are hurting my tongue and lip. It feels like it is cutting through my flesh. I'm sitting in Dr. Dillon's office, awaiting my follow-up visit (one week) after the jaw was wired shut.

Please give me good news!

Later....

No such luck. We have another visit next week!

Monday, October 24, 2011

This morning I have so much to do. Nicole is coming to get me to the county office to handle my paperwork.

I need to figure out all of this Family Medical Leave Act(FMLA) stuff, and then I have go to the Social Security office in order to file for disability for Theron and Corinne. Additionally, I am going to fax my paperwork to the doctors. No, I think I will just wait until I see both of them: Dr. Dillon on Friday and Dr. Henderson on November 7, 2011.

Yesterday, Jemel, Terrence's former boss came by to fix Corinne's bed, and then he and Benny, Terrence's friend, came back to put up the rail to help Corinne walk up the steps when she gets home! It was one of the doctors' requirements in order for her to be released. My little girl will be home soon!

Lord, thank you for your gifts of provision. The school gave me tons of food for the kids and for myself—as well as money to help with bills and other living expenses.

I got a huge basket from fifth grade with pudding, Jell-O, juice and soups! How thoughtful! I am so grateful. I am so thankful to be among the living, and I am so thankful to be loved by so many.

Love,

Kimya

Facebook on October 26, 2011

The prayers of the righteous availeth much! The great news is Corinne came home yesterday. According to the docs, she has months of rehab still to go. We all know that God has the final say so.

Additionally, about a quarter of her skull is missing, they are making her a new one so that when her brain has healed completely, they will replace her skull. So, I am asking everyone to continue to pray for complete healing and restoration, safety (no falls before her skull is replaced; it can be very dangerous), and for a successful surgery and recovery. Thank you for your prayers and support at this time.

Monday, October 31, 2011

Dear Lord,

I just found the letter Terrence wrote to Corinne before the shooting.

I am still questioning why would he do something like this. Why would he try to kill us?

Not sure what to do with the letter.

I just found the CD and the VCR tape of the wedding as well. I'm feeling a little sad right now. I never would've dreamed that someone I loved so much could turn on us like this.

Looking at his picture, I ran my fingers lightly over his face and smiled. It seems that the "Terry" I married is so different from the "Terrence" that shot us. He could be such a good husband at times... rubbing my feet, taking good care of me when I was sick, stretching me out after I exercised, bringing me flowers "just because," giving me sweet cards, making passionate love to me, sharing his fries, having tea parties with Corinne, teaching her how to build and tear down houses, and treating her like a princess...

Later...

I ended up throwing everything away. I'm still looking for my wedding and engagement pics. I'm going to throw those away as well.

Love ya,
Kimya

Spotlight on Recovery – Cutting All Ties: One of the most important things you will need to

do in order to move on after abuse is to cut all ties to your abusive ex and the past. You may feel an urge to show him how strong you are after the relationship, offer advice, check on him to see if he is alright, say how much you miss him, get an explanation for his abusive behavior, and/or share your sentiments of forgiveness. Don't. The best way to get real closure is no contact ("Closure,"2013).

- **Avoid phone contact**: Delete his number from your phone. If you feel the need to call, find someone else you trust to talk to, put the phone down and do something else you love to do, or put it in another room and walk away.
- **Purge social media**: Unfriend, unfollow, and repeat. Do this for your ex and his friends and family you are still connected to on all social media sites. Resist the urge to look at his page to find out how he is doing. You may even have to block him to avoid seeing his pictures and/or stories pop up in your news feed or timeline.
- **Write a letter**: If you feel you need closure, you can write a letter to him. Say everything you'd like to say to him in person, but put it in letter form. When you are finished, burn the letter or tear it into tiny pieces.
- **Give away or trash belongings**: I once went through my closet and grabbed every purse, piece of clothing, jewelry, and even his

Christmas stocking, put them in a large trash
bag, and gave them to my local second-hand
shop (but, I put the diamond ring in the
collection basket in church). I took every
letter, card, and picture and put them in the
trash can. It is important to clear your home of
every reminder of the past.

- **Supervised Child Visitation:** If you share
children and they have visitation with the
non-custodial parent, consider using a
visitation center. Ask your local domestic
violence organization and/or the courts for a
referral. You can pick up and drop off the
child(ren) in a safe location.

What Can You Do About It?

Philippians 3:13 Brothers, I do not (a) consider myself
to have taken hold of it. But one thing I do: Forgetting what
is behind and reaching forward to what is ahead

God has a wonderful future in store for you, but you
have to be willing to let go of your hurtful past and trust
Him to bring someone new into your life that loves and
respects you in the way you deserve. He cannot "pour new
wine into old wine skins," so allow him to renew your mind
and heart in preparation of for your new life.

Pray: Father God, turn my heart towards you and open
up my ears to hear from you like never before. Heal my
heart from all the pains of the past, so I can be a new
creature in Christ. Prepare me to be a good mate for the
person you have chosen for me. In Jesus's name, Amen.

Chapter 19: Mama Bear

I was lying on the couch when Theron got home from school. He stood directly in front of me with a look of pure terror in his eyes.

"He has unfinished business, Mom."

"What are you talking about, T.J.?"

"Mr. Terrence. He can get out, Mommy. He could come and kill us all."

"Little boy, Terrence is not getting out. He sleeps in a one-man cell guarded by sheriffs twenty-four hours a day. I promise you're safe, sweetie."

He walked over to me to where I was lying down on the couch and put his head on my chest.

"Hugs and stuff, Mom."

I just held him as long as he would let me. I wanted him to feel completely safe. I couldn't let him know that I lived in daily terror too.

He smiled at me and went upstairs to play his video game for a while before he did his homework so I decided to write a diary entry.

Diary Entry Thursday, November 3, 2011

Dear Lord,

So much has been going on since Corinne came home.

On Tuesday Night (October 25), she was very concerned for her safety. She said she didn't feel very safe and wondered if I was safe as well.

On Wednesday, October 26, Courtney's birthday, she told me a story about what she THOUGHT happened at Egleston, but it was something that happened the day of the shooting. She said the police officer kept asking her to sit down, but she wanted to catch the bus. I told her the incident didn't happen, and she said, "Yes it did." And that I was there.

But, as you know Lord, that didn't happen at Egleston. It happened after she was shot.

I am so worried about what I am going to tell her. The doctors say that she is not ready to know the truth. How am I going to tell her that the man she loves so much did this to her?

Yesterday, I took her to the pediatrician. Dr. Sulton was very concerned about how Theron was taking everything. And as you know, he is not taking it well. He had one counseling session with the child life specialists at Scottish Rite. He still needs more counseling. I am very worried about him. I need to reassure him and spend some special one-on-one time with him. He lives in constant fear that Terrence is going to break out and try to kill him too.

Later that night, Corinne had a very bad headache. Headaches were her new "normal" since the shooting, but this one seemed exceptionally bad.

I heard sobs coming from Corinne's room. "What's wrong little girl?" I asked as I walked into her room.

Rocking and holding her head in pain, Corinne shouted, "Somebody better tell me who did this to me!"

I was advised by Dr. McCann to tell her what happened to her the next time she asked about it. So I did.

I took a deep breath and sat down next to my sweet girl on her aqua blue comforter. I held her in my arms, began to do the rocking for her, and prayed silently before I spoke.

"Corinne."

"Yes, Mommy?"

"Do you remember the morning I took you to daycare and you only had one shoe on your foot?"
"Yes."

"What else do you remember from that day?"

"I remember going to sit down on that thing by the door to put my shoe on...I don't know what else."

"Well, Corinne, I need you to know something. Not long after you sat down on that ramp, Terrence shot you in the head."

"What?!" she shouted, pushing away from me.

"And he shot me, too...multiple times."

"Mommy, why would he do that?" She started shaking her head and wailing in despair. "Mommy!" she screamed, putting both hands over her ears and rocking more powerfully. "What did I do wrong? Was I a bad little girl? Was it because I didn't clean my room?!"

She dropped her hands and looked up into my eyes. "Corinne, it isn't..."

She cut me off. "He doesn't love me anymore?!"

"No, baby. No, baby. It isn't any of that. You did nothing wrong. Nothing at all. Don't you dare blame yourself for any of this," I whispered to her. I wrapped my arms around her again and continued to rock her and sing: "You are my sunshine...my only sunshine..."

Corinne was very upset by it all. I told her that I'm sure if he were thinking clearly that he never would have done that to her.

She looked up at me and stopped crying long enough to ask me, "What about you? Would he have done that to you if he were thinking clearly?"

"I don't know, baby. I'll be right back ok?"

I went downstairs to get some pain medication, juice, and analgesic cream to rub on her head.

When I returned to her room, she quickly took the pills and drank the juice. I sat down on her bed and rubbed the cream on her forehead, temples and around the back of her head. I then turned off the light in her room because sometimes light made her pain worse and I thought it would help. I walked back over to sit on her bed and rocked her until she went to sleep. This would be our routine for months to come.

Diary Entry – Later that night

Lord,

Well you know that I don't know the answer to that question.

I don't know if he still would've done it to me— thinking clearly or not.

I just rocked Corinne in my arms, in the dark in her bed until she went to sleep. That's when my tears came...slowly...then streaming...

We'll talk more later!

Love,

Kimya

On Sunday, I was lying on my bed reading some magazines that my coworkers, Talesha and Sabrina brought to me. For the first time, I felt like I could exhale a bit and do something to give my mind a break from all the serious stuff I had going on in my life.

Much to my surprise, I received a phone call that would change the rest of my day.

"Hello."

"Him, Kim. This is Flossie."

"Hi, Mrs. Roberson. How are you?"

"I'm fine, baby. How are you? How's Corinne?"

I told her about all the milestones Corinne had been hitting and how she was doing much better than all the doctors thought she would do.

"That is wonderful, baby. We been praying for all of ya'll: My school, the teachers, the kids in my class, and the people at the church. You wouldn't accept any phone calls from us when you were in the hospital so other people have been tellin' us how you were doin'. I knew ya'll were going to pull through. God's got you."

"Yes, Ma'am. He does."

"Kim, can I ask you a question?"

"Yes."

"Was Terry ever mean or violent to you before he got the sarcoidosis?"

"No, ma'am. He wasn't."

"That's what I thought. I knew it was that sarcoidosis that was making him act like that. Kim, we didn't raise Terry to act like that. He is always helping people. He got a good heart. I just knew it had to be the sarcoidosis. You know I been reading up on it, and they say that sarcoidosis in the brain could cause you to go crazy."

"Ms. Roberson, Terrence didn't have neurological sarcoidosis. It only affected his lungs."

"No. Uh-uh, Kim. Remember that doctor he was seeing in Atlanta asked you if he got mean when he got it? That's because it can travel to the brain. I read it and that's what I believe happened."

I couldn't think of what to say. I couldn't believe what I was hearing. I actually took the phone out of my ear and looked at it so I could see if this was really happening or if I was in the Twilight Zone somewhere. I placed the phone back to my ear.

"Kim, baby? You there?"

"Yes, ma'am."

"You know I talked to his Uncle, too. He say Terry been telling him all kinds of things he had to do when he was in that military. The stuff he said Terry had to do when he was in there is enough to make anybody's head turn, you know?"

"Ms. Roberson, I've got to go. I am not feeling well. I am very sleepy from all the medicine they've given me." I began to cry silently.

"Ok, baby. You go and get some rest. I feel like since God gave you and Corinne a second chance, He is gon' give my baby a second chance, too. He a good boy. You know?"

I found it difficult to breathe through the wires and control my crying at the same time.

"Ms. Roberson, I tried to tell you over and over again what Terrence was doing." I sniffed and took a deep breath.

"I told you I was scared of him." I took deeper breaths because I found it increasingly hard to breathe. I couldn't seem to finish what I truly wanted to say to her.

"Now Corinne and I are doing better, but we both have a long road to recovery." At this point, I almost felt like I was going to pass out. I kept taking deep breaths to talk to her. It hurt so bad – my heart and my lungs. My heart started pounding in my chest like a racehorse.

"Not to mention the counseling we both have to go through. All three of us..."

Mrs. Roberson interrupted, "I know how you feel, Kim. Thanksgiving is coming up and we won't have him at the table. It is going to be so hard for all of us," she explained through the tears I heard from her on the other line. "You and Corinne are better off than Terrence right now."

I don't know how I got off that phone with her, but I ended it cordially and began to hyperventilate.

I went downstairs where Sandy was working in my living room, and she walked with me outside so I could get some air.

When I was finally able to calm down, I came back inside, crawled into my bed, and began to write while hot tears slowly trickled down my face.

Diary Entry Sunday, November 6, 2011

Dear Lord,

I just got off the phone with Terrence's mother, and I'm feeling extremely overwhelmed. I can't believe that she said the things she said. She tries to justify his actions.

Lord, it seems to me that she wants her son out of jail. It seems to me that she didn't really care about me or Corinne. That hurt me so badly.

Monday, November 7, 2011

Dear Lord,

Thank you for your many blessings! Corinne came home from day rehab today with her green card! Yay! She is now able to walk without someone holding her gait belt. Go, Jesus! I also found out too that the grand jury has indicted Terrence on five counts: two conspiracies to commit murder, two aggravated assaults, and one use of a weapon in the commission of a crime.

Thank you, Father Jehovah, who calls all things into being.

While I was feeling down about having to be under general anesthesia to have the remaining two bullets removed, I also received the wonderful news that the wires in my jaw would be removed. Yay!

After spending four weeks with my wires, let's just say that I am so happy that they are being removed.

*Not being able to eat what I've wanted to eat
has really worked to try to break my spirit. Just
watching other people eat what I've wanted has
moved me to tears. You know that first week was
"hell." I remember when Courtney said, "Auntie, are
you ok?" I wasn't. Between bouts of extreme nausea
and diarrhea, I felt very low physically and mentally.*

*I remember sitting in Corinne's family meeting
at Scottish Rite totally embarrassed because my
stomach was making noises like water running
through pipes.*

*I remember sitting in the attorney's office when
diarrhea struck me again and again.*

*And today, after listening to Pattie LaBelle's
version of "A Change is Gonna Come," I realized that
you love my children and me so much. You've
watched us go through so much, and it seems that
you are saying that it is our time to walk in the
sunshine.*

*I feel like blessings are overtaking us. Thank
you. Lord! Lord, thank you for watching over my
children and me. Thank you for loving me.*

*Lord, thank you for Michael. He's coming
tomorrow night to make sure he is there for the
surgery on Wednesday. He's been there for me for
every surgery and for the craziness that culminated in
the shooting. Lord, I love him so much. Thank you for
sending me a love so sweet and so pure. Thank you
for sending me someone to love me BACK.*

Just this past weekend alone, you've filled me with such joy and inspiration by bringing my Aunt Denise here. She has always been an inspiration to me. She's written a fabulous book. It is so well done and so professional looking, and the words contained within are so inspiring. I am definitely writing a book when all of this has passed.

Thank you for my life, my children, my sister, my niece, my family, and my friends. Thank you for providing for us and blessing us.

Use me for your purpose. I want to be your illuminating light for many. I want to draw people to you. I want to help women leave abusive relationships. I want to be an advocate for autism and TBI (traumatic brain injury). I want to be a champion for you, Father. I am available to you.

Tuesday, November 8, 2011

Dear Lord,

I am sitting in pre-op this morning, waiting to be seen. As you know, I have to have a surgery tomorrow to remove the bullets. I am putting all my trust in You. Today Mike is moving to Covington. I am really excited about that!

Later....

As I am preparing for bed, I have a lot on my mind. I am praying that I will be 100%. I look at myself and see a broken woman. My body has not healed, and I keep requiring more repair.

My teeth have been destroyed by the shooting or these wires in my mouth. I don't want to smile for that reason. Please give me the resources to allow my mouth, my entire mouth, to be fixed.

Thank you for the Olive Garden and the clothes I purchased today. Lord, a size 10? I have always been a size 14 or 16. Really? Thank you so much!

Thank you for the time I got to spend with Michael tonight. It was great lying in his bed, watching him unpack his bags. He carefully hung up each item in his closet (color-coordinated, of course) and folded up his other clothes and neatly placed them in his drawers. I saw this as a strong symbol of his love for me. It made me love him all the more.

Thank you for Sandy and Courtney being here with me Thank you for Theron and Corinne. Thank you for being the love of my life!

Ode to God

He's strong and mighty,
Tall and powerful.
He's loving and merciful,
Full of love and grace.
I love the Lord
With all my heart.
It's Him I trust and
Won't Ever depart
Because He loves me
So effortlessly.
Simply put, I love the Lord.
Love, Kimya

Diary Entry Saturday, November 12, 2011

Dear Lord,

This morning I woke up and decided to drive myself to the hair salon. Technically, I'm not supposed to be driving yet, but I am at the point where I am tired of waiting for somebody to help me. I can't sit around here helpless.

On Wednesday, I had part of my surgery. Because they couldn't get my mouth open all the way, the anesthesiologist gave me some Versed and local anesthetic. Dr. Henderson promptly removed that bullet. In fact, they acted as though it was some kind of baby. I heard them say, "We got it!" The nurses echoed their triumph, and I asked to see it.

It was gold/bronze in color and had a rounded edge. I asked if I could keep it, and they told me, "No."

Apparently, Investigator Pilgrim, one of the lead detectives on my case, went to pick it up the same day. Anyway, I was pretty happy about that. They said the other one is located below my left clavicle, which Michael told me is my collar bone.

I don't know what the plans are for getting that one. I guess I'll just have to wait and see until I go to my appointment next week.

Well, as you know, on Tuesday, Dr. Dillon removed the wires that connected my arch bars. On Wednesday, the left side of my face began swelling. Due to the increased swelling, he put rubber bands back on the arch bars for four more weeks.

I was absolutely devastated.

Corinne's special dinner is Sunday; her birthday is next week, and Thanksgiving is the following week. I WANT TO EAT!

Michael was such a big help. Several times when I wanted to cry, he either hugged me or made me laugh by cracking jokes. He is so wonderful!

Then I really hurt his feelings when my cousin and his wife came by for a surprise visit.

The doorbell rang and Michael opened the door.

"Well, well, well, if it isn't that pretty girl, Miss Kim Motley."

"Hey Vinson," I said and began to get up off the couch.

"No, sit down. I am going to come over there and hug your neck."

His wife came in behind him and hugged me, too.

"Now who is this young man?" Vinson asked.

I paused a long while and said, "This is my very best friend on the planet."

I watched Michael's face drop as he held out his hand to shake Vinson's.

"How you doing, man? Michael."

They all sat down, and we had a conversation filled with talks of God and laughter, but Michael was noticeably bothered by what just happened. I did not acknowledge him as the man in my life.

Diary Entry Saturday, November 12, 2011 (later that day)

Dear Lord,

I am so concerned about what other people think about me and how I'm representing you. People think it is too soon for me to be in a relationship, but I need him. I love him. I really don't ever want to hurt him. He means the world to me.

Thank You so much for sending him to me. Please give me the strength to stand up for what I believe to be right. He is a very important aspect of my life, and I want it to remain that way. Please bless our relationship so that we are always loving toward one another and we're not doing anything to hurt one another.

Diary Entry Tuesday, November 15, 2011

Dear Lord,

On Sunday, Springfield Baptist Church celebrated Corinne Williams Day! It was quite spectacular! When we brought her into the children's church, the room exploded with applause, cheers, and chants for Corinne. They had a special chair of honor for her and everything.

I felt so honored to have the love of so many strangers. Corinne just beamed. She was so proud that everyone thought so much of her.

Why did they care so much? We aren't even members of this church.

Afterward, we were escorted into the main sanctuary. Pastor Lee spoke about how you need a touch from God and how to obtain it.

I have definitely received a touch from You, and I am so thankful for your many blessings.

Diary Entry Wednesday, November 16, 2011

Good morning Father Jehovah,

I was reminded this morning just how comforting Psalms can be. Ms. Stegall, the speech pathologist at my school, sent me some scriptures about God protecting me (oops! I meant to say "You") and how You will take care of my enemies. I found some really good scriptures to meditate on for a while.

Ever since the financial aid people took the $500 from my account, I've been worried about some things. However, Stegall encouraged me to cast my burdens upon you (Psalm 55:22). My burdens include provisions for Corinne's rehab services, insurance premiums, household bills, victim's assistance compensation for loss of income, medical expenses, counseling, or Social Security Insurance benefits for medical and monthly stipends for Corinne and myself.

Please deliver me from unforgiveness. Please deliver my loved ones from unforgiveness. Please help me to forgive Terrence, his mom, and my relatives for judging me instead of loving me. I don't want to be walking around with any resentment or anger towards anyone. Help me to forgive my bosses as well. I felt like they didn't understand or they didn't want to help me when I reached out to them.

*Now back to casting my burdens on you...I
need enough food for everyone for Corinne's birthday
party.*

*So much to be thankful for and yet still worried a bit
about this party. Lord, I believe. Now please help the little
part of me that still doesn't believe.*

Diary Entry Thursday, November 17, 2011

Dear Lord,

> *Thank you so much for today's happiness. It
> could have been so different. Today Corinne is
> celebrating her eleventh birthday! It is only because of
> you that she is here. Hallelujah! I can't wait until this
> weekend when we get to celebrate even more.*

Later...

> *Today the Criminal Investigations Division threw
> Corinne a surprise birthday party. Investigator
> Pilgrim called me on Monday to tell me that they
> needed me to come in to the office for further
> questioning.*

I was trying to do some cleaning around the house
when I heard the phone ring.

"Hello."

"Hey, Kimya. How are you doing girl?"

"I'm great, Amanda. How are you?"

"I'm good. Listen. Lieutenant Wolfe needs you,
Corinne, and her grandparents to come in for some
questions."

I started wringing my hands together as anxiety
began to rise in me.

I cleared my throat a bit and asked, "Amanda, is everything ok? What is it? Is it something they can use to get him off?"

"No, girl! Just come in so we can ask you a few more questions."

"Okay, Amanda. We will be there."
"Okay, great! I will see you on Thursday then."

Upon hanging up the phone, all my old fears came back.

Would they be mad that I was talking to Terrence while we had the restraining order like Terrence threatened me they would?

Were they going to arrest me, too?

Would his attorney be able to use that against me?

Would he get out?

Let's just say that I didn't have much peace in the next three days.

Lieutenant Wolfe met us in the lobby and escorted us to a large room in the back of the sheriff's office. He tried to make small talk, but I found it increasingly hard to concentrate on what he was saying or asking me because all I could think about this impending "questioning."

Imagine our surprise when we walked into that room and many members of the sheriff's office shouted, "Surprise!" Wolfe and Pilgrim could not attend Corinne's party on Saturday so they decided to throw her a surprise party there!

She had balloons, flowers, cake, and loads of presents. She received Braves hats, a Braves jersey, a Braves jacket, a Falcons jersey, art supplies, and her favorite: a Princess Tiana doll.

I could not believe the love, compassion, and empathy we were receiving from all of them. God is truly wonderful, and it was only going to get better from there.

On Saturday, we continued the celebration by throwing Corinne a huge birthday party. Her birthday was more than just a way to celebrate her eleventh birthday. It was a day to rejoice what a great miracle God performed in her honor.

She had a Supergirl, spa-inspired party with all of the accompaniments. Bringing the birthday party festivities to fruition was a small miracle in itself. I had not been working for the past two months; therefore, I had no income to support her party. But I promised a grand party that everyone would remember, and God helped to make sure that she got her party just the way she always imagined it.

Nicole surprised me with the venue for our party. She and her husband are co-pastors at The Branch Worship Center, and they agreed to let us use the church for Corinne's party. I couldn't think of a better place to hold the celebration.

To further my excitement, back in October, Tonya Beacham, owner of Diva Spa Girlz parties, offered to throw Corinne a party free of charge! Can you believe that? All I had to provide was the food. I thought that would prove to be a challenge due to my economic limitations, but God had other ideas in mind. Corinne's dad and several people joined in to help purchase the food or other party goods, and the party did not disappoint. It truly took a village to bring the party to reality!

The guests arrived at 3:00 p.m. to the sounds of Mindless Behavior—her favorite group. The large room was transformed into an oasis of pink and turquoise blue (her favorite colors) with large balloons, banners, and streamers covering the walls.

There were stations located around the wall that enticed the children to participate in the assortment of spa offerings, including a waiting area filled with teen magazines and lounging chairs, areas for manicures, pedicures, facials, and a glamorous makeover table, brimming with cosmetics that would turn any ordinary girl into a princess for a day.

The menu was all of her choosing: cheeseburger sliders, nachos, chicken sliders, hotdogs with all the trimmings (cheese, chili, onions, peppers, sauerkraut, and coleslaw), Buffalo wings, pasta salad, blue punch, and a pink and blue Supergirl cake prominently displayed in the center of the table. Corinne had been on a feeding tube for many weeks and had gradually been introduced to solid food. She talked about this menu for weeks!

Guests were instructed to arrive in super hero costumes, and for hours, we were surrounded by everyone from Supergirl to Recycle Girl.

I ordered a Wonder Woman shirt and cape for me, a Green Lantern shirt for Theron, and a Batman shirt for Michael. With the help of Ms. Deneen Moss, Corinne's Girl Scout leader, Deneen's daughter, Christine, and Tonya, we designed a spectacular costume for Corinne to wear. She wore a white t-shirt with a grand pink and blue "S" exhibited proudly on her chest. She also wore a pink and blue tutu to accentuate the colors in her shirt. She wore pink tights and pink and blue Air Jordan's to round out the look. She looked absolutely adorable! The day couldn't have been any more perfect.

Corinne was surrounded by family and friends from school and even her best friend, Chelle, whom she hadn't "seen in forever".

Upon arrival, each girl was given a treatment card to wear around her neck to indicate which three services she would like to sign up for. They also had gorgeous white robes to wrap themselves in as they were being pampered. Even though each region of the church was busy with partygoers, the manicure table was by far the most popular, and believe it or not, it had the girls refusing food in order to get their manicures completed.

After all services were completed, the lines began to form for the food! Since I could not eat anything (thanks to my newly wired mouth), I happily helped Kiki, Lynn, and Andria serve the food to our partygoers. Everyone sat and dined for what seemed like hours as I tirelessly greeted guests, refilled cups, and smiled for a dozen pictures.

As soon as the food was over, we had a magnificent fashion show to show off all the superhero attire.

When it was Corinne's turn, I wasn't quite sure what to expect. She had always been so quiet and shy before.

Would she even want to walk across that stage?

I didn't want to overwhelm her or insist that she do something that under normal circumstances would make her feel uncomfortable so I decided to go over to the line to have a talk with her.

"Hey little girl! I am so proud of you. Are you having a good time?" I asked her with a ginormous smile of pride on my face.

"Yes, Mommy. This party is so awesome!" she answered with an equally big grin.

"Corinne, you don't have to do the fashion show if you don't want to. I know you are shy, and if you are too scared to do it, everyone will understand."

My Supergirl responded quite confidently, "No, Mommy. I'm not scared. I can do it. Watch me."

My eyes lit up with surprise yet there was still some lingering sense of doubt.

Could she really do it?

"Ok, Corinne. Girl, strut your stuff across that stage!"

When it was her turn, Corinne ascended the steps to the stage and walked proudly to the middle to showcase her outfit. To everyone's delight, she did an impromptu dance in the middle of the stage and then exited to the far right.

My mouth dropped! I was so shocked to see my once shy little girl act with such bravery on that stage.

It made me remember one thing that Dr. Chern said about my daughter when she was in the hospital. I remember her grandmother told me that Dr. Chern said that Corinne would never be the same Corinne that we knew from before. The bullet had exploded and liquefied a part of her brain that controlled her personality and executive function (her ability to remember, learn new things, and plan for the future).

Well, it was definitely true! She was NOT the same Corinne that I knew prior to September 20. She was a new creature in Christ, and God replaced the old, shy, introverted Corinne with a new vibrant, outgoing little girl full of sunshine, personality, and sass.

Corinne received so many gifts, including clothes and art supplies. Her favorite gift was the Nintendo DSI given to her by Deneen Moss, who took up donations to provide it to her.

Diary Entry Wednesday, November 23, 2011

Good afternoon Jehovah,

> *I'm feeling very overwhelmed with a decision I have to make. Aungelique Proctor from the news came to my house about an hour ago and wants to do a story on Corinne and me. No one knows but You about what should happen. Jehovah, I don't want to do anything to jeopardize my case.*
>
> *I do not want fifteen minutes of fame.*
>
> *I want to do Your will, and I want your name exalted in the land.*
>
> *I want my story and Corinne's story to bring glory to only you.*

I want to be your voice on the Earth. I know that Aungelique has a job to do as well.

First and foremost, I am Your daughter. I am not self-seeking. On September 20, You made me a new creature.

Second, I need to protect Corinne, Theron, and myself and other people from Terrence. I guess I really don't have to do that—that's Your job. You did a great job protecting us on that day.

I just don't know what to do. Help me decide, Father. Should I do the interview with her or not?

In Jesus's name I pray, Amen.

Spotlight on Recovery – Your Support

System: An awesome support system is vital to rebuilding your life after an abusive relationship. Sometimes this isn't always possible. Either your ex isolated you from your family and friends (you couldn't talk or visit with them much if at all unless he was present), OR your family and friends walked away from you because of the relationship and the number of times you kept going back. Sometimes, your family and friends do not believe you were being abused because of the relationship they have with your ex. If you are one of the blessed ones that still have your support network in place, that's AWESOME! If you are not, there are some things you can do to create one:

- **Support groups**. Many counties have domestic violence support groups. These groups can help you build a connection with other people that have been through abuse. The facilitators can provide some real hands-on tips for healing and building new healthy relationships. Ask your local domestic violence crisis line, shelter, or agency for referrals.
- **Domestic violence advocate**. You can find a shoulder to cry on, an ear to listen to you, and an informed person to help guide you on your path to wellness. Advocates can help you complete paperwork, go with you to court, and connect you to legal and/or social service agencies to help you get back on your feet.

- **Pastors or spiritual Leaders**. Ask your faith leader if he/she has experience in dealing with domestic violence. If the answer is no, make sure you are also connected with a domestic violence advocate. Domestic violence advocates can help you with the practical side of abuse, and your spiritual leader can help you with the spiritual side. A spiritual leader praying with you and giving you scriptures can be very comforting.

- **Me, myself, and I**. Never underestimate leaning on yourself as a valuable tool. Find a good self-help book about domestic violence, go to classes, take up a hobby you always wanted to try (i.e. dance or cooking classes), start exercising and eating right, and make a vision board to help you capture your future in a positive way ("Support System, "n.d.).

- **Psychologists, counselors, and therapists**. As a victim of domestic violence, you may experience bouts of depression, anxiety, and post-traumatic stress disorder. A professional counselor can offer crisis intervention, referrals to community resources, and safety planning. Specific therapies should focus on empowering you to begin to feel confident in yourself and your decisions again (Crabtree-Nelson, 2010).

- **Online communities:** Looking to your social media networks can be an awesome source of support as long as your friends/connections are positive. Don't be afraid to delete or block anyone who is being negative about your healing. Be very careful about comparing your life to the lives of the people you are connected with on social media. Remember they only show you the highlight reel.

What Can You Do About It?

*Hebrews 13:1 – 3*¹Let brotherly love continue. ²Don't neglect to show hospitality, for by doing this some have welcomed angels as guest without knowing it. ³Remember the prisoners, as though you were in prison with them, and the mistreated as though you yourselves were suffering bodily."

It is important to lean on your support system when rebuilding your life after abuse. Don't forget the most important component of your support system: Your heavenly Father. You will be more effective when pairing that support with prayer and spending time with your Him daily.

Pray: Father God, please show me my armor bearers and my support system in this journey. You have my permission to sever all ties to any unholy alliances. In the name of Jesus, I pray. Amen.

Chapter 20: Tired of Being Afraid

Diary Entry Thursday, December 1, 2011

Dear Lord,

I cannot seem to sleep for some reason. I am not worried about anything, but I guess I just have a lot on my mind. I apologize for not writing sooner, but it seems my life is full of so much, and I'm not making the time I need to write.

I'm tired of people telling me how I should feel. I am angry, scared, and lonely in all of this.

I don't want to go to trial!

I don't want my kids to have to be put on the witness stand.

I just want all of this to be over!

I feel like he's winning. I am sick of his ass!

Today was his arraignment, and his attorneys asked for a continuance. They are waiting for a psychological evaluation, which has not been completed yet.

The assistant DA said Terrence plans on pleading not guilty due to a mental illness. I wish I could click my heels and say, "There's no place like home" and be whisked away to my happy place where shootings and trials are not in existence. I want to be free. Free, Lord!

Right now, I feel so lost. I just kept crying today—tears I've kept in for so long. They are burning and stinging my face. They are from a place deep down inside that I often keep hidden from the world.

I just feel so overwhelmed with responsibilities. Daddy is sick and has been transferred to a nursing home. They say he is declining.

Corinne is crying; she is sad about rehab and school. She is ready to go back.

Theron is upset about his workload in school.

I'm overwhelmed with my OWN emotions. I am dealing with the shooting, parenting, and being a daughter, a girlfriend, and just being me.

Lord, I need some peace, PLEASE!

Diary Entry Sunday, December 11, 2011

Lord,

I am feeling all types of emotions this morning. The church put together a celebrity basketball game to raise money for our recovery. I don't know why, but I am even scared of it!

I am scared of my reaction.

I am afraid to get up and speak in front of people.

I don't know how I am going to react or how people will receive that reaction.

232

I am scared of how to say thank you and, again, the reception of the thank you.

Lastly I am afraid of people coming out of the woodwork trying to take or manipulate me for the money.

Actually, I am just scared of pretty much everything. I am full of fears this morning.

I am afraid of the trial.

I am afraid of Theron and Corinne's emotional state now, at the trial, and beyond...

I am afraid of the type of sentence he will receive, facing him, my divorce proceedings, and how that whole procedure will work.

I am afraid of the fate of my jaw. Will the swelling go down or will I need surgery or two more months of this wiring?

I am afraid of gaining weight. I have always been a big girl and felt fat and unattractive. I am finally liking myself.

I am afraid of my relationship with Michael. I love him, and I know he loves me, but I'm scared of my ability to maintain the level of cleanliness he desires. I am afraid of our disagreements over how I parent and discipline my children. I am afraid of how he compares me to his exes and whether he will let these things keep him from being with me.

I am afraid of Theron's progress in school or lack of; is he making any? Will he graduate on time?

I am afraid of Corinne's lack of progress; will she be retained in 5th grade?

233

I am afraid of going back to work. Can I be happy there? Can I handle the workload?

I am afraid of the cars that pull up on my street and I don't know who they belong to.

I am afraid of White Chevy Silverados.

I am afraid of my own reflection in the side mirrors when I reach in my car to get something.

Is that enough? As I told You, I am just full of fears, but I thank you for the scriptures on fear that you've given me that bring me comfort right now. So, I thank You that Your perfect love casts out all fear, and I thank You that You have NOT given me a spirit of fear, but of love, power, and soundness of mind.

Monday, December 12, 2011

Yesterday was wonderful Father! I thank You for giving me the courage to speak in front of the congregation yesterday. A group of complete strangers wanted to show us Your love through their generosity. They celebrity basketball game raised over $11,000 for us.

I wanted to be able to speak Your truth.

I wanted to touch people for You.

I wanted people to be encouraged by Your love for me.

Most of all, I wanted You to receive the glory.

Lord, You are awesome! Thank You for the money! Thank You for the courage! Thank You for the love you've shown me through people

Diary entry Wednesday, December 14, 2011

Good evening Jehovah,

The past few days have been wonderful and eye-opening. Thank you for the pen, journal, and gift card from Alvinette Maultsby, my coworker. I am sure I will get many weeks of writing out of them!

We talked at length about her friend that died two months before my shooting at the hands of her husband. She said the husband shot the woman and then himself. Wow!

Even Kiska, another complete stranger turned friend, told me that there were several cases of domestic violence against women in the months leading up to the shooting, and none of the women lived. Wow, Lord! You really showed me Your love and Your favor.

Why didn't You save those other women?

I know I didn't do anything right in all of this.

Why did You choose me to live?

Why my daughter?

Well, since You did save me, please show me what You want me to do with my life. You preserved our lives for a reason. Please bring the right people into our lives and send the wrong people out. Please continue to show us Your grace and mercy.

Lord, I have a BIG decision to make tomorrow. Since my face is swollen, Dr. Dillon told me that I needed to either go ahead and have the surgery, which means getting my face and/or neck cut again, OR to be wired for two more months. I DON'T WANT THIS!!! Truth be told, I'm still waiting on a miracle from You. I've been wired for a LONG time. I am thankful that I am now a size 8, but I don't want to be on liquids for two more months, Lord.

I don't want to have surgery, either.

I do not want Dr. Dillon to cut my face.

Why can't I already be healed?

Why can't all of this be over?

It seems really overwhelming. I have a deep-seated anger and hatred for Terrence that seems to grow daily. It feels like it is taking over my heart. Watching Theron's challenges, Corinne's challenges, and my challenges is too much for me at times.

Sometimes I wish he were dead. Is that wrong, Lord?

Yesterday, I went to see my therapist. I think we will make a lot of progress. She said she feels good about talking to Theron and me.

I need to find some funds to help me send Corinne to the therapist that specializes in traumatic brain injury. Children's Healthcare of Atlanta recommended her because she helps children come to terms with having a Traumatic Brain Injury.

On a good note, Corinne graduates from day rehab next week (on the 22nd). She will then continue with outpatient therapy for speech and physical therapy. They want her to go to the hospital/homebound at first, where her teacher will come into our home and give her lessons, then attend school half days, and transition to whole days. Lord, only You know what's best for Corinne. Please restore EVERYTHING about her. Rewire her brain better than it was before.

Guess what? On Monday, I will be a divorced woman. Yay! I know You hate divorce, but a little piece of me wants to believe You are doing a dance in heaven like I'm doing here in my room. "Go, Jesus! Go, Jesus!"

Please ensure that he does not come to the divorce proceedings and everything goes smoothly.

After the conversation I had with Michael, I am back to being afraid of our relationship again. I don't know what to think of his comments. I really need to know how he feels about my children. Does he love my children? Is he counting down the time until they leave? How does he feel about them? All I know is that I'm scared, Lord. I am trying to figure out who I am again. I am trying to make sure Theron and Corinne are healthy. I am trying to be a good girlfriend. It appears that I am failing at everything. I don't want to make any mistakes. I am tired, Lord. Just tired.

Diary Entry Thursday, December 15, 2011

Good evening Lord,

Today has been full of many events and emotions. This morning, I woke up, and after I dropped Corinne off at the bus stop, I went to see Dr. Dillon. He wired me up for four more weeks, but he will check it in three.

I have been very sad today. I don't want to miss any more holidays. Michael says that I am here, and that's all that matters.

I know he is right, but I WANT TO EAT, Father!

I love everything about Christmas, especially the food.

I am tired of pudding, Jell-O, soup, Gatorade, PowerAde, milkshakes, smoothies, and anything that goes up a straw.

I missed Thanksgiving, although I still had a wonderful time with my family and Michael.

I don't want to be ungrateful. I couldn't stand it if You felt unappreciated. I thank you, Jehovah, for my life and that I get to see another Christmas and New Year's Eve with my children, my sister, my niece, my dad, and Michael.

Michael found my diary and read it. He was hurt about what I wrote in there about his feelings toward my children. I found myself apologizing over and over again. He is so wonderful to forgive me for doubting at times. Jehovah, I am just so scared. I know that my marriage to Terrence was for a much greater purpose than "happily ever after," but I need to know that this time Michael and I can be happy with one another. He has already said, well, I guess we both said, we are not getting a divorce so please touch our relationship and guide it from courtship to marriage. Please bless us to give each other many years of happiness.

But, Lord, I am so scared. What if we're not right for each other?

I am so thankful to you for Michael and how he stood by my side, but sometimes there is still this lingering doubt.

On another note, Theron has been working really hard on studying for exams over this past week. He still isn't motivated to help around the house, but his attitude has gotten somewhat better. Thank You for a change of attitude.

Please help Theron experience You in a special way (that doesn't involve death). I want him to love You like I do (if not more). I thank You that my season of losing is over. Thank You for Theron's laptop. Just thank You for loving and keeping me.

Diary Entry Monday, December 19, 2011 @ 9:20 a.m.

Dear Lord,

I am sitting in the courtroom on the day of my divorce. Everything is so uncertain. Margaret and I sat down outside the courtroom initially. We weren't sure if we were able to come in or not, but when we saw other people come in, we came in.

Lord, my heart is beating like a racehorse. I am so scared, and I don't know why. I don't know what is going to happen today—in this moment—but please, please let this end today and end well. I have this sneaking feeling that he is going to come in here. I am not ready to face him yet. Jesus, help me. I thank you that your perfect love casts out all fear. I thank You for keeping me in perfect peace because as I sit here, I will keep my mind stayed on You. Well, my heart has stopped beating so fast at least.

Margaret and I have talked about everything from the types of watches people word to courtroom trials (and Terrence's arraignment—he asked for a continuance for a mental health evaluation), but I wish this along with everything related to Terrence was over. But if YOU be for ME, who dares to stand against me?

Judge Andrews just did the call of calendar. He called everyone's name from his list and asked us to stand and say present when called. When it was my turn, he asked me if Terrence was going to be present. I told him no.

"Kimya Roberson, please take the stand. "My knees were shaking as I left the wooden bench to approach the judge. I felt like every eye was on me as I cleared my throat to get ready to speak.

"Good morning, Ms. Roberson," Judge Andrews said in a surprisingly warm voice.

"Good morning."

"You're here this morning to seek a divorce from Terrence Roberson?"

"Yes, sir."

"Was he served with the divorce papers?"

"Yes, sir."

"So, he just decided not to come then?"

"I'm not sure, sir. He's in the Rockdale County Jail." Judge Andrews looked over the paperwork. His eyes got really big as he read the bottom of the document where it described the shooting in full detail.

"Oh, I see. Okay, did you get married on September 16, 2000?"

"Yes, sir."

"Did you separate on or about January 31, 2010?"

"Yes, sir."

Technically, he was kicked out of the house on January 31, and we hadn't lived together again, but I was hoping and praying the judge wouldn't ask me if I'd seen him or talked to him.

Terrence had scared me so much about this possibility for months. Terrence told me the judge would make me stay with him or I would go to jail if the judge knew I had talked to him.. He said these things in an effort to make me stay with him.

I took a deep breath and answered, "Yes, sir."

He didn't ask me anything else about it. *Yes!* I cheered inside.

Judge Andrews then looked at me over the top of his wire-rimmed glasses and asked, "Is there a chance for reconciliation?"

"NO! Umm, no, sir" was the answer that came out of my mouth, but I wanted to say, "Hell no! Hell NAW! Oh no!" I had a few other statements I could've used, but I knew it was not appropriate for court.

He then paused a while as if he were pondering something serious and whispered, "So, how's your daughter doing?"

I told him about all the progress she was making. I told him she was out of the hospital and was being bussed to rehab daily.

He told me how happy he was to hear that and that he had been praying for us.

I whispered my thanks to him, and then he said the words that made me feel like I'd won a million dollars: "Divorce granted!"

I was elated, Lord! I turned around and smiled the biggest smile at Margaret; I felt so relieved. I have agonized in my mind what I thought was going to happen in that moment. And You have been so faithful.

Tuesday, December 20, 2011

Good morning Lord,

Thank you so much for allowing me to see this day. It is the third month anniversary of the shooting. I know an anniversary is yearly, but I feel I need to thank you every month that I am alive. Everything is great! Yesterday You gave me a divorce without any problems.

So many good things happened yesterday after that! When I came out of court, the surgery coordinator called to schedule Corinne's surgery. They are going to put her left side of her skull in on January 6. I don't have to live in fear anymore of her having a serious injury and hurting her brain.

Margaret and I went on to Don Tello's to have celebration margaritas. I removed my rubber bands and ate some cheese soaked nachos and drank a rainbow margarita. I know I wasn't supposed to, but just this once shouldn't hurt. I'm tired of liquids! They both were delicious.

I came home to take a three-hour nap and when I woke up, I discovered that my mortgage payments are going down by $50 for next year. Thank You!

6:36 p.m.

Corinne and I are very weepy this afternoon! I am not sure why we are crying, but, Lord, I just need some peace. I was so happy earlier, and now, for some unknown reason, I am sad again. In this very moment, I am not happy. I feel every emotion.

I want to run away from this place and forget everything that has happened here. Sometimes it feels like it is going to take too much effort to rebuild. I don't want to be here. I feel the fear of him in this space. I have irrational fears at times: fears of him breaking out of jail, his Momma or daddy hurting Corinne or me, or simply reliving the event over and over again. I just want to get away.

Then, at times, I am not sure about Michael. He is having his own set of problems and how can I help him or vice versa when everything is so screwed up? Both of our lives are crazy right now for different reasons. I feel as though when I talk to him, the things I say are not right. He constantly corrects what I say, even when I'm trying to encourage him. He says he is a realist, but it seems at times he can be very pessimistic. I can be the <u>extreme</u> opposite—very optimistic. Well, right now, one of us has to be strong for the other one, and it seems that neither of us can do that. I don't know what to do.

All I know is that I am very sad, and I need You to do something. I was just explaining to Michael that I either need You to give me the peace that passes all understanding in order to live in his house OR give us the financial blessing to be able to move to another place, whether it is in this city or another. I don't want to live here anymore. It seems like everywhere I turn, something reminds me of him. Lord, what do You want from me? Covington or Savannah? Or some other place?

Right now, I feel at a loss about my life decisions.

Can Michael and I be happy together?

Am I supposed to live here or somewhere else?

Please help, Lord.

Love,

Kimya

Diary Entry Thursday, December 22, 2011

Good morning Jehovah,

Today is Corinne's last day of rehab. She is graduating! Yay! I will write more later to let You know about that.

I've been thinking about titles for my book. I've been thinking of "Enough is Enough" or "All I Did Was Turn My Head. What do you think? Or "When You Are Full, You Push Back From the Table." I don't know.

Last night, we went to Jemel and Marie's house. Jemel is Terrence's former boss, and he has made us a part of their family. Marie asked me to bring Corinne over to help the grandkids put up the tree. When we arrived, they'd already put up most of the tree. Corinne was able to put up one ornament, but she mostly popped bubble wrap with the other kids.

Jemel gave Theron and Corinne pizza and soda. Oh, and hot wings. Of course, they enjoyed that.

Jemel spent some time trying to talk to Theron, but Theron always tries to sit where I am. I really want him to try to spend more time with men. Michael and Harry said they were going to spend time with him. I am looking forward to that.

Anyway, it felt very strange being at their house. The only time I've been over there is when I was with Terrence. I kept feeling like he was going to walk in the door at any point. It wasn't a scary feeling. In fact, being at Jemel's house with Terrence were typically good occasions. So I felt kind of sad. I reminisced a bit about some happier times, and now I am still wondering how he went to hating me so much...

That's one of the reasons why I am feeling anxiety about my relationship with Michael. I love him, he loves me, and everything feels good. I don't ever want it to turn dark. He is a wonderful man— loving, generous, nurturing, sensitive, and communicates well. We like the same things and have similar goals for the future. Jehovah, let YOUR will be done in Michael's and my life.

Spotlight on Recovery – Posttraumatic Stress Disorder (PTSD):

Have you experienced feelings of betrayal, abandonment, and constant fear of people, places, and situations? You are not alone. Studies show that 31- 84% of women that have been victimized experience some sort of PTSD. In fact, the more life-threatening the situation, the higher the incidence of symptoms. PTSD can manifest itself as flashbacks, nightmares, increased anxiety, hypervigilance, trouble sleeping, digestive issues, and emotional numbing. As a way to cope with the symptoms, you may have become depressed, got involved with drugs or alcohol, or had thoughts of suicide (Cohen, Field, Campbell &Hien, 2010). There are positive ways of dealing with PTSD. They include:

- **Exposure therapy:** This technique puts you in the midst of people or situations that cause the PTSD episode. For me, the smell and sound of fireworks put me right back in the scene of the shooting. So for the 4th of July, I went to a neighborhood where they had fireworks displays. I cried and smelled and heard the fireworks until it no longer made me cry. I took my power back.
- **Medicine:** Certain anti-anxiety medications may help with the symptoms of PTSD. Ask

your mental health professional if it is right for you.

- **Support groups:** Groups offered by your mental health professional or local domestic violence organization can help you feel like you're not alone. Talking about your feelings can help you feel confident about your choices again and find comfort in sharing your thoughts about the abuse.

- **Self-care:** Taking time for yourself by getting enough sleep, exercising, eating right, getting a manicure, or having a chill day by watching a funny T.V. show can help you calm down and refocus your thoughts and feelings on the positive things going on in your life. You can also simply sit in the car, listening to your fave songs, singing as loud as you can, while eating an ice cream cone (can you tell that I'm talking about myself?).

What can you do about it?

Psalm 23:4 Even when I go through the darkest valley, (a) I fear no danger, for You are with me: Your rod and Your staff (b) – they comfort me

You do not have to be a prisoner of fear. Do not allow fear and anxiety to keep you from enjoying the life and love you desire. Along with seeking help from a domestic violence advocate and counselor, begin to find scriptures that speak to you about fear. Write them down and meditate on them. Pray them aloud whenever you feel anxious or overwhelmed. Before you know it, God will fill you with love, power, and soundness of mind. And poof! PTSD will be a thing of the past!

Pray: Father God, fill me with your perfect love and throw away all fear from me. Help me to deal with the number of emotions I am going through right now. I thank you for all my trials and tribulations. I know you are using them to shape me into the person you've called me to be. Help me to find a therapist and the perfect remedies to help me deal with my fear. I am looking forward to the day I walk in complete restoration. In Jesus's name, Amen.

Chapter 21: Happy New Year! I Guess...

January 2012

Diary Entry Wednesday January 4, 2012

Dear Lord,

So much has happened since I wrote in here last...

Michael and I went on a mini vacation to Savannah right after celebrating Christmas with the children. Corinne stayed at Sandy's and T.J. stayed part-time with his grandma and part-time by himself. Since we've come back, Theron has really been acting out. Apparently, while we were gone, Theron took Michael's PS3 controller and used it without permission. We'd already spoken about touching other's belongings when he played Michael's game without permission.

Diary Entry Thursday, January 5, 2012

Dear Lord Jehovah,

There is just no way I will make it without You!

I am so overwhelmed. I don't know how to handle everything.

See, when Theron took Michael's controller without asking, I thought it would be an appropriate punishment to take away his games the same number of days he took the controller.

Theron was mad about the games so he wanted to mess up the oil so we couldn't have dinner. While I was frying fish, he poured cold buttermilk into the oil in an attempt to prevent me from cooking. Instead, the oil flared up into brief flames.

We began intensive family intervention and counseling again, which required an overnight stay for Theron. I am so glad that we did the counseling because it was revealed that he was really hurt and angry about the shooting and didn't know how to deal with his feelings.

I didn't even mention that I spent all morning at Egleston's pre-op for Corinne's pending skull surgery. I am mentally and physically exhausted! Please help me! There is so much to do...even today, and I am tired Lord. Your daughter is tired. But I will praise Your name when I'm down. I will praise Your name when I'm up. Hallelujah!

Facebook post:

Since I last posted a comment, Corinne has graduated from Day Rehab. She now has to go to speech therapy and physical therapy once a week for one hour. If it is God's will, she should be ready to return to school full-time in mid-February. God is awesome!

Corinne will have her skull replacement surgery tomorrow. Please be in prayer for her.

My son has been having a hard time emotionally since the shooting. He feels as if God does NOT exist because of what happened to his sister and me. He is under attack—please pray for him too.

Thank you for your prayers and words of encouragement.

Diary Entry Friday, January 6, 2012

After weeks of rehabilitation in Day Rehab at Scottish Rite, Corinne is now scheduled to have her skull replaced. When she was shot, the left side of her skull was splintered, fragmented, and was rendered unusable. A few weeks before the scheduled surgery, we went to Egleston to have CT scans of her head done. Dr. Chern would use these images to make a plastic model of her skull and use it to replace the piece that was missing.

I am frightened about the possible outcomes of them going back into her brain. Would the progress she's made thus far be hindered? Would we have to begin rehab all over again? Surely those things were possibilities. My anxiety is only intensifying as January 6th draws closer. I keep telling myself that all of the people that were there when she was first injured would be there with me to offer me comforting words as I awaited her second brain surgery. I wouldn't have to endure this alone.

On the morning of January 6, 2012, I arrived at Egleston at 5:00 a.m. for her scheduled surgery. Having had the pre-operative visit a few days earlier, we were ushered to the back rather quickly to begin the process of preparing her for surgery.

She changed into her hospital gown and began to cry a little bit. Her optimism was now being replaced by fear. "Mommy, is it going to hurt?"

I reassured her that it would not because they were going to give her medications to alleviate her pain, but she continued to cry.

"Mommy, this isn't fair. Why is this happening to me?" she inquired through her bevy of tears.

"Corinne, I don't know why this is happening to you, and no, it isn't fair. I agree with you, but what you have to understand is that this procedure has to happen so your brain has the protection it needs. Don't you want to play basketball or ride your skateboard again?"

"Yes."

"Okay then. Let's do what we have to do in order to get this done. I'm going to be right here with you."

I wiped her tears with my hands, kissed her face, and gave her a big hug, holding her in my arms like I used to do when she was just a small toddler.

Just then, Dr. Chern and his team arrived to discuss the details of the surgery with us. After he explained that the surgery would take approximately three hours to complete and someone would call me after each hour to inform me of the progress, he asked if we had any questions.

Corinne raised her hand as if she were in school and asked, "Will you have to cut my hair off again? I don't want it cut anymore because it has just started to grow."

Dr. Chern chuckled at this statement and informed her that he would be extra careful about cutting her hair and would only cut as little as necessary to implement the procedure. After leaving, her nurse came into the room and gave her some medicine to help her relax. Corinne went to sleep not long after, and I was ushered into the waiting room for her surgery to begin and started to write.

Diary entry:

Dear Lord Jehovah,

I just got a visit from nurse Mary Gates who said she operated on Corinne when the shooting happened.

Two ladies in hospital scrubs approached me while I was sitting in the waiting area and writing in my journal.

"Hi, are you Mrs. Williams?" said a lady in teal hospital scrubs.

"Umm, no, ma'am, but I am Corinne Williams's mom."

"Great!" She turned to the lady behind her and said, "Kim, it IS her!"

"Listen, I am one of nurses that assisted in the surgery when your daughter was shot." She grabbed the other lady by her waist and pulled her close to me. "This here is Kim. She was there, too! And one other person, Al, was there, but he isn't here today."

"Hi. It's so very nice to meet both of you!"

"No," Kim interjected, "WE are so very happy to meet YOU!" She held out her hand to shake mine.

Mary started again. "Listen to me. God has something great for Corinne in this world. There is something miraculous that happened in that room that day."

"Yes," Kim said. "You are not going to believe this story. We were at the end of our workday, getting ready to wind down from the night before, when we got a call to come and assist with the ten-year-old child with a gunshot wound to the head. All the neuro nurses were occupied and couldn't assist. Kate, who was the head neurology nurse, was the only one available."

I listened with increasing anticipation.

"Now the rest of us are the head nurses in other areas: urology, spine, and anything from the waist down." She started laughing. "Your daughter had the best of the best in the room that day, but none of us had a clue about the brain. When we were first called into the room, we were bumping into each other."

Mary started laughing too and said, "Remember? They were calling us the Four Stooges."

"Yep!" Kim continued, "We didn't know how to prep or what to do. Kate and Dr. Chern were doing their best to direct us, but, girlll, we had no clue."

"None," Mary added.

"But girl, when Corinne arrived through those double doors, it's as if Jesus entered the room. All of a sudden, we just KNEW what to do." She started slowly waving her hands in a circular motion. "Everythang was moving like clockwork—like everything just fell into place." Kim's eyes widened.

The phone rang next to me, interrupting her story.

"Hello."

"Hello, Ms. Motley?"

"Yes."

"This is Kate. I just wanted you to know that everything is going well. Corinne's vital signs are stable. We are moving right along."

"Okay. Thank you so much!"

"No problem. I will call you again as soon as Dr. Chern is finished."

"Thanks so much!"

I was feeling so elated and started thinking to myself: *Thank you, Jesus! Thank you, Jehovah! Thank you, Holy Spirit!*

Mary interrupted my thoughts and asked, "How's our girl?"

I explained everything Kate just told me. Mary and Kim gave each other a high-five and talked about how strong Corinne was. She was fighter.

"Girl, let me finish this story," Kim continued. "After the surgery was finished, we all looked at each and said, 'What just happened?' We couldn't explain what we did or how we worked. We were back in a state of total confusion."

"Yes," Mary added. "Even the doctors said we did a great job. All we could do is look back and forth at each other in disbelief. I couldn't tell you from that day to this one what we did exactly."

"At this point, Dr. Chern told us that your daughter wouldn't make it. Taking a look at her then, no one believed she would. He told us that he wanted us to go down and talk to the family and let them know," said Kim.

257

I couldn't say one word. I was picturing this whole scene playing out before me. I was in total amazement.

Mary continued, "All I could think was I wouldn't be the one to tell them. I just couldn't do THAT. It was the longest and saddest walk ever."

"When we arrived in the waiting area," Kim explained, "Dr. Chern told her grandmother, father, and the rest of the family there that your little girl wouldn't make it through the next twenty-four hours. They all asked questions and when Dr. Chern left they all began to cry."

"Kim and I didn't know what to do when Kim said, 'We should pray with them.'"

"So," said Kim, "we all grabbed hands and made a circle in the waiting room of the hospital and began to pray for your little girl. We both walked away feeling really sad, but we said we were going to check on her every day. We couldn't believe that she recovered!"

At this point, all of us were crying and hugging each other. Mary pulled some Kleenex from the box on the table and handed it to each of us.

"That's why Mary said we should try to find you when we saw that Corinne was here this morning for the skull replacement. We were both scared that you wouldn't want to talk to us."

"No," I said while wiping my eyes and blowing my nose gently. "I am so glad you came to talk to me. This blessed me so much. You have no idea." I started crying again.

I was so moved by their story. It seemed God was with my baby from the minute she left me until she arrived at the hospital...just like I prayed. After they left, I finished my diary entry...

> *God you truly are awesome! The nurses want to be a part of her life from now on. They say Corinne is their family and she is their baby. They want to know about everything she is doing in school, in sports, dances, and they even want to be there for graduation and when she gets married! Thank You, Lord, for taking such good care of her. Thank You for taking such good care of me. You are awesome and worthy to be praised.*
>
> *Love,*
> *Kimya (will write more later)*

9:51 a.m.

> *Just observing how everyone else is here with people and I'm here alone! I am not sure why no one wanted to be here during her surgery, but it is a little lonely, but, at the same time, it isn't so bad*
> *. Thank You for having me remember the laptop and having those ladies talk to me. It made the wait easier.*
>
> *Michael says that everyone else was here when I couldn't be so now it's my turn.*
>
> *But still it just feels like they don't care.*

10:40 a.m.

> *I finished talking to Dr. Chern about 10:30. He said the procedure went very well, and he expects her to do very well. In fact, they finished EARLY! Go, Jesus!*

Now I'm downstairs having a caramel
*Frappuccino from Starbucks. The lady was so sweet;
she made it just the way I wanted it. I am going to
call a few people now and await the moment when I
get to see my pretty princess. In case I don't tell You
often enough, thank You for giving me my baby back.*
10:20 p.m.

*Lord, I've finally made it to my sleeping pod,
yes! It is a little area where parents can rest while
their children are in the hospital. I am so very tired! I
didn't get much rest last night. I had so much on my
mind, but tonight I am going to rest.*

*You gave my child and me a second chance.
After today's surgery, she is done. She is now on the
road back to being the Corinne who enjoyed sports
and dancing.*

*Today was hard being here alone, but I was
able to make it through. I don't know why their father
did not come to see Corinne or T.J. today, but I can't
change him. I can only be the best mother I know how
to be. We'll talk more tomorrow. I am so sleepy.*

Love,

Kimya

Diary Entry Saturday, January 7, 2012 5:02 a.m.

Dear Jehovah,

*I went in to see Corinne this morning, and her
head is considerably larger.*

I spoke to the doctors. They said that because she did not tolerate medicine and because she was vomiting and not eating food, they were going to keep her another day. The good news is that swelling is normal, and she will move to a regular room today.

1:10 p.m.

When I went downstairs to eat, I found some carrot soufflé and some turkey chili. It was blended so smoothly it was easy for me to suck up the straw. Yay! Today was a good cafeteria day!

I still feel kind of upset that I do not have any support from her family. No calls or visits. It hurts, but I feel like my children are only a priority to my sister and my friends. Theron is in crisis and could use some parental support. Lord, I need some help. This single parenting is hard!

Monday, January 9, 2012

Dear Lord,

Thank You for waking me up this morning. Thank You that Corinne's recovery is moving in a positive direction. Lord Jehovah, thank You for sending Michael to spend time with Corinne and me. Jehovah, Michael really is a wonderful man. He is very supportive, loyal, and just there when I need him. As you know, I felt very alone when we first got here on Friday.

Thank You that Margaret, Corinne's grandmother came here to support me on Friday and Saturday. She came up after surgery on Friday and brought Stephanie and her sister to see Corinne on Saturday. I was worried for nothing.

261

Corinne got moved to room 5238 on the east wing on Saturday afternoon. Lisa was her nurse when we arrived, and Lisa was her nurse from 7 p.m. through 7 a.m. She was wonderful! Lisa was very attentive to Corinne's needs. Her blood pressure dropped and was low throughout most of the night. Lisa kept checking on her, getting IV fluids, administering meds, and just being extra kind and gentle with her. Lisa's bedside manner was superb amongst her peers. I plan on writing a commentary card for her before I leave.

When the doctors came to see Corinne Sunday morning, they said they wanted to keep her an additional day because of her pressure and she wouldn't eat much. Throughout the day, Corinne's eating improved and so did her blood pressure. That was a relief. So we will find out what the doctors say this morning, BUT she should go home.

Right now I feel kind of numb about my situation. I am not really sure about what I should be doing or thinking at all. I told Michael yesterday that I feel so overwhelmed because my plate is sooo full.

Before the shooting, dealing with Terrence's erratic behavior and threats of violence seemed overwhelming. Although annoying I felt as though I could handle it and could cope with it.

Now the thought of being hurt by him is off my plate, but just look at what's been added: my emotional and physical well-being, Corinne's emotional and physical well-being, Theron's emotional well-being, Daddy's physical well-being, whether or not or how I am going to be able to go back to work, and financial responsibilities. It is just too much at times.

So, Lord, I'm leaning and depending on You. I can't make it through the storm without You.

6:45 a.m.

One of the doctors on Chern's team came to see Corinne. He said she should be getting ready to go home later today. The problem is her face is now completely swollen and both of her eyes are shut.

I am worried about how she is going to handle this emotionally when we come home. Of course, the doctors say the swelling is normal, but they don't have to deal with a whining girl, and she SHOULD whine. Who wants to go to bed with the ability to see only to wake up and not see? Lord, help her and me.

On top of that, I cannot use food to comfort me at all. I am hungry and want something GOOD. Dr. Dillon put the wires, not the rubber bands, back on my mouth on Thursday. He said he couldn't trust me because I kept taking them off and eating whatever I could fit in my mouth. Due to my non-compliance, I have four more weeks. Finding foods I can eat has not been the easiest task.

I will talk to You more later, Jehovah. I just ask that as I cast my burdens upon You so that You will make my load light. Please handle all my problems. I'm putting them in Your box. In Jesus's name, I pray.

My World

Spinning out of control or so it seems,
But I look to Him as he shines his BEAMS
Of light on me to make my path illuminating
so I can stop whining, pining, and ruminating.
All of the problems seem to engulf me
instead I will sit, pray, love, and flee
to His arms that hold me
near and cry in his chest
as he begins to steer
Me into the path of
destiny that he has
prepared just for Me!
I love you Jehovah, Jesus, and Holy Spirit!

Diary entry Wednesday, January 11, 2012

Dear Jehovah,

Thank You for my delicious smoothie this morning. I mixed mango, pineapple, and yogurt together to try to make something appetizing.

Thank You that Theron opened up to me about his feelings last night. He cried and talked to me about his fears. He said that we were living in the house with a murderer the whole time, and we didn't know it.

He says that he keeps flashing back to the shooting, and although he wasn't there, he says that he can see it. Theron talks about times when Terrence would act violently toward him.

I have a meeting with Valerie, my therapist today. It is my second one. She wants to meet Corinne as well. I'm not sure what we are going to talk about, but I will let You know more later.

My aunt Denise says that I'm a good mommy, but, Lord, a lot of times I question my own judgment and some of the choices I've made. I don't think my children have had the best childhood possible.

Jehovah, don't I deserve to have a happy family life with loving, well-balanced children and a sweet, supportive husband?

I want a good life, Lord.

I still want that!

I don't want it exclusive of You; it is NOT more important than my relationship with You. But if it is Your will from this point on, I would love to have a drama-free family life. I just want to live out the rest of my life in peace. I want the same for my children. I do not want them perpetuating the same toxic cycles we've seen on both sides of my family. In Jesus's name, I pray.

Love,
Kimya

Diary entry Wednesday, January 11, 2012 6:16 p.m.

Dear Lord Jehovah,

I am so angry, frustrated, and feel just plain crazy right now. I feel like I am not in control of anything and everything is in control of me.

Corinne's teacher came today. Her name is Mrs. Ravenell. Corinne did very well with math but began to struggle with the reading. She says she is ready to go back to school, but she lacks the motivation to persevere. If today is any indication of her expected performance, she is in trouble. I don't understand her at all. She is giving Ms. Ravenell the business. She won't cooperate with her classwork. She won't cooperate with the homework Ms. Ravenell leaves for her.

Right now I don't feel like I have enough power within me to fight it at all. I think that if I go to the gym and work out, maybe some of this agitation I feel will go away. I don't know.

Several times a day, I feel like just crying. I feel very weepy. I just feel down.

Theron is still saying that he is having flashbacks from the shooting.

Thank You, Lord! Corinne just came downstairs to do her homework! Hallelujah!

I should be able to help them both, but I feel weak and inferior right now.

On top of that, Theron just wrote this one page summary for school of the horrible things that have happened in this community to include the shooting and how this has contributed to him not believing in You. Why Lord? This is all too much for me to handle.

I feel like I am losing my grip or my strength. I don't have much left. I just want to cry or scream or something. I just want to release it all, but I can't.

I think I'm slipping into depression.

Please help me! In Jesus's name, I pray. Amen.

Diary Entry 7:44 a.m. Thursday, January 12, 2012

Dear Lord Jehovah,

If I didn't tell You already, thank You for Dr. Lederman. I think Theron will "gel" with this guy because he is very experienced in Asperger's syndrome and he is an older white gentleman. Theron respects older men.

I started feeling sad again (just a little) after our visit to the counselor, but I was able to get it together later. It would be nice if I could put away the Christmas stuff and workout— along with taking Corinne to outpatient therapy, helping her complete her homework, going to Theron's school, going to Walmart to buy folders for receipts, and taking his glasses to Pearle. I have a lot on my plate. Please help me, Lord.

Last night, Corinne woke up and began vomiting. Please let that mean nothing at all. In Jesus's name, I pray. Amen.

Diary Entry Thursday, January 19, 2012 around 12 something a.m.

Dear Lord,

First and foremost, I want to thank You for the change in Theron. He has definitely made a 180-degree turn for the better.

He hasn't been fussing when I ask him to do something—no making sounds by sucking his teeth and no talking back! He's only been saying, "Okay." That is one of the best gifts ever given to me.

On top of chores and little jobs I ask him to do, he has been completing assignments in a timely manner. Theron has been studying and doing homework without even being asked to do so. Hallelujah! Glory to the name of Jehovah! On top of that, he's being really sweet to Corinne and me. Go, Jesus!

. Thank You that I've been able to go to work out every day this week. Thank You for helping me complete all of my daily tasks. I have sent paperwork to Theron's school and took Theron's glasses to have them repaired. You are so awesome!

I put all of those things in my prayers last week, and You answered them all. You've even made my depression disappear. I'm in a much better mental state this week!

Thank You for the nap I had earlier today.

*Jehovah, thank You for sending my
stepmother, Emily to us as well. She has been so
helpful to me. She's been cooking dinner for the
children every night and been cleaning the kitchen. I
promised to make a sour cream pound cake for her
before she leaves, and You've gotta help me to
remember that. We've had great talks, and she's been
a source of encouragement for the children and me
. On top of that, she loves Michael! (What's not
to like about him?) Thank You that she took down my
Christmas things and put them in boxes But anyway,
as Saturday approaches, I hate to see her go.*

*I had some unresolved and buried
anger/resentment toward her that I didn't realize I
had until she got here. Having her here helped me to
resolve all the unforgiveness. I am so glad that she is
my stepmother and can be here for the children and
me now when we need her.*

*Lord, I am asking You to create in me a clean
heart and renew within me a right spirit. Cleanse me
of all iniquity. I don't want bitterness or resentment
to take root in my kids or me toward anyone.*

In Jesus's name,
Kimya

11:27 A.M.

Dear Lord,

*I am at Dr. Dillon's office for my appointment.
I am praying in two weeks these arch bars will come
off my teeth and there will be no swelling. At that
time, I will have had them on my teeth for four
months.*

I'm not really sure why he wants to see me, but I will just be glad when we can move past the bars and onto teeth replacement.

On my way to see Dr. Dillon, Michael and I had a disagreement or a miscommunication. I think that we have these misunderstandings quite a bit. I will say something that he takes the wrong way or he will say something that I will take the wrong way. A lot of times, I feel as if I'm walking on eggshells. I don't want to feel this way, and I don't want him to feel this way either.

At 2:00 today, there is going to be a motions hearing. I wanted to be able to go or send Margaret or something, but I'm not sure if it is even necessary.

Lord, rule and reign inside that courtroom. Send forth all of Your warring angels to force out, cast out, and keep out all demonic spirits that war against my family and me from everywhere we are, everywhere we are going, everywhere we've been, everywhere we will be, and everywhere we are being represented.

I ask You that justice is served in our case, and Terrence receives the punishment you feel he deserves.

I pray that Theron, Corinne, and I no longer live in fear from this day and all the days of our lives.

I pray that You remove the people from our lives that are not meant to be there or who will cause us problems later. I pray that only people YOU send will be a part of our lives.

2:59 p.m.

Right now, we are Mt. Zion for Corinne's speech appointment.

She gets tired of coming to these appointments and says she's ready for school. A lot of times she says it's unfair that she has a brain injury, but it is great that at this office I was able to show her two other children that have the same cuts on their heads like hers. Maybe that will help her realize that she is not the only one going through this.

Love, Kimya

Monday, January 23, 2012 9:15 a.m.

Dear Lord,

It is raining cats and dogs outside. Apparently there is a tornado in Alabama that is moving here. The sky is all gray, and the clouds are ominous. They match the mood I woke up with this morning.

I just felt eerie and dark.

I went to the gym to try to clear my head, but it really didn't help.

I still don't know what happened at that motions hearing on Thursday, and I don't know if or when we are being placed on the trial calendar.

Not knowing stuff is making me CRAZY! Jehovah, I just want all of this to be over. O-V-E-R. I can't stand it! I feel like my life is at a standstill, and

I cannot move forward without him being sentenced. Everything is on hold. I don't know when I can return to work.

Diary Entry Thursday, January 26, 2012

Dear Lord,

Thank You so much for waking me up this morning

Thank You for food for my children to eat, gas for my car, and money to do what needs to be done while I'm not working.

Lord, my room is a mess. Right now I feel all over the place with my emotions, and my room is a reflection of that. I feel like a ticking time bomb ready to explode. Dr. Michael said that when we bury our feelings, anger (especially) comes out in other ways. I guess I've been burying something because more and more I feel agitated.

I'm beginning to get snappy with the children.

My work is not getting done.

I feel anxiety about a number of things. I am worried about the trial, my job, and my relationship with Michael.

I am burying a lot of things that I'm not telling other people. So I'm going to tell You. Maybe if I get it off my chest, I'll feel better. Right now I feel beat down by my circumstances—trapped and imprisoned! After what I went through with Terrence, I never wanted to feel that way again, but I do.

Jehovah, I do not like working at my school anymore. I feel as if I am walking on egg shells all the time. I do not want to return to a place where I cannot make a difference, where my voice is not heard, and where my efforts go unnoticed. I want to be in a career that I love where I am respected and celebrated and where I can make a mark on this world. I don't feel like my place is at my school anymore.

As far as the trial and Terrence goes, every week, I've been getting stronger and stronger. My fears are slowly dissipating, and I'm actually becoming stronger mentally than I was before. Thank You, Lord, for helping me to identify my victim mentality and helping me to overcome it.

Love,
Kimya

Chapter 22: Hills and Valleys

Diary entry Wednesday, February 1, 2012

Dear Lord,

Today I feel like such a loser. Corinne's homework is not completed, my room is still not clean (it's a hot mess), and I missed Theron's appointment this week for Dr. Michael; I am not getting my stuff done! On top of that, I am going to be expected to go back to work soon. Ehh!!!! Help! I feel like an emotional wreck. I feel as though I can't get it together, and Dr. Ramesh won't give me any ADHD meds. He says I need to get back to a point of normalcy before he does. What the hell is that? Now it seems that all I want to do is sleep.

Days like today, I feel like I hate Terrence for what he's done to her. Corinne really struggles with school and homework. Yesterday, they put her in special education classes. She told me today: "I have missed half of the school year, and now I am stupid."

I hate him for what he's done to her!!! School is hard enough in fifth grade without the added frustration of a brain injury. And then she has to make the transition to middle school like this.

On February 11th, I took Corinne to the doctor to see Dr. Chern. This was her last visit. Dr. Chern looked at Corinne with amazement.

"Corinne, promise me that you will be a neurosurgeon when you grow up."

Corinne started laughing. "I will think about it, Dr. Chern."

Dr. Chern then turned to me. "Please, I want to always know what she is doing. I want to know how she is doing in school and in life. You know?"

"We promise to send you pictures, letters, and cards to let you know what Corinne is up to. We promise! Right, Corinne?

"Yes."

He then turned back to Corinne and opened a box he had in his hand.

"Corinne, this is the model of your skull we made when we took the picture of your brain. You remember that?"

He handed it to her.

"Yes. It's blue! My favorite color. So my bones are blue now? Will it glow in the dark in my head when the lights are out?

"No, Corinne." Dr. Chern started chuckling.

"So you mean my head won't glow in the dark?"

"No, sweetheart." He started laughing even more.

"Usually, I give the skull models to the patients once I've finished with their care, but I want to ask you a very serious question."

"What?"

"Corinne," I interrupted. "It's 'yes,' never 'what.'"

"I mean, yes, Dr. Chern," Corinne answered.

"Will you let me keep yours?" He scooted his rolling stool closer to her.

"This skull reminds me why I come to work every day. I want to use it to teach other doctors about your procedure and recovery. More than that, I want to put it on my desk and be reminded of you and your strength."

At that, tears started to roll down my cheeks.

Without hesitation, Corinne told him that he could keep her skull model. She even promised him that she would THINK about becoming a neurosurgeon.

"Dr. Chern, how long before she can get back to life? She wants to go skateboarding and is looking forward to the summer so she can go to Six Flags."

"Corinne, I promise in two weeks you can ride a bike, go to recess, skate, get your hair braided, have P.E. and go to Six Flags!"

Corinne jumped off the examination table and gave him a high-five.

We left the hospital feeling the best we had felt in a LONG time.

Tuesday, February 21, 2012

Good morning Father Jehovah,

I haven't written in here in such a long time, and I believe that it is starting to show in my spirit and my body.

I am stressed to the max about several things, and, Lord, I desperately need Your peace.

To begin with, my relationship with Michael is on the rocks. I feel that we are both bringing our emotional traumas into our relationship, and it is suffering because of it.

I am a rebellious teenager. That's what Valerie called me. I think because on the day I was shot, I feel as if I were born again or recreated. So now I am in my rebellious teenager stage. I don't want anyone to tell me what to do, including him. I want to be able to let You lead the way and enjoy the triumphs of MY decisions. I've let people tell me what to do my whole life. Letting other people make decisions for me is giving them control. And I don't want to be controlled anymore!

Additionally, I have been reading this great book about domestic violence. It is called Why Does He Do That? *It is a wonderful resource in understanding the mind of the abuser. But the problem is now I am seeing abuse EVERYWHERE!!! I am so hypervigilant about protecting myself. I don't want to be hurt again.*

I want to be with Michael, BUT ONLY if that means we can be married in a peaceful, loving, happy, mutually satisfying relationship.

We've both been through the ringer in our fair share of abusive relationships, Jehovah. I guess I want You to say, "Not this time." I want to feel like this time, my relationship is going to last forever.

I want You to bless our relationship with all the good things. I want us to be able to go forth and love one another and not be hurt by one another.

We are definitely at a crossroads. You've said that we are to be each other's mate. How do we withstand the transition period? When do we get to the point of being healthy?

Diary Entry Thursday, February 23, 2012

Dear Lord,

Last night, after Michael and I argued about what he feels I was saying or doing, a bunch of thoughts came over me, and I am scared of being hurt Lord. Deeply scared of hurt. Terrence said that even if I left him and got with someone else, I would be hurt. He was right! Although I know that Michael's intentions would never be to hurt me physically or cheat on me, it seems that simple things hurt me.

Arguing hurts!

Misunderstanding hurts!

Always having to defend my thoughts, motives, and actions hurt!

I love Michael, and I am at the midpoint of trusting him. Some days I feel like I can trust him completely. Some days I wonder if I can.

I am ready to heal!

Heal!

I am ready for love, respect, and peace. Am I being naïve about not wanting to argue about stuff?

I seek to bring closure to our misunderstandings, and it seems as though he keeps using arguments and misunderstandings from the past to bring up over and over, and it only causes the drama to perpetuate.

At one a.m., I acknowledged to the world via Facebook that I am in a relationship with him. It appeared on both of our pages. In the past, *he felt like I was trying to hide him because I was ashamed of him. That is not true! Will my relationship with Michael affect the trial like everyone says? That is all I am concerned about.*

I am trusting in you, God, that the post is the beginning of his trust in me and my trust in him. I am ready to move forward. I am ready to leave the past behind. Lord, I am not perfect, and neither is he, but I want us to try to love one another without hurting one another.

Diary entry Tuesday, March 27, 2012

Dear Lord Jehovah,

I need You to send forth all of your comforting angels now. I am hurting so badly. This is just too much. You said You won't put more on me than I can bear, and, well, I can't bear this.

Lord, I am not healed completely emotionally. I am still hurting and trying to make sense of my marriage to Terrence and how he came to shoot me. I've had to deal with watching him try to murder my daughter and watch her fight for her life back.

I've watched my son slip in and out of depression. I've watched Corinne have another relapse because she got hit in the head with a basketball on Friday, and now Michael doesn't want me anymore because I don't clean up and maintain a house well. Well, at least it seems like that is his problem with me. He says it isn't, but it seems like this is true. He says he can't take my going back and forth and indecisiveness.

He promised me that he would not hurt me or allow anyone to hurt me. I found safety in that statement, but he wants what he wants, and that is not me.

Terrence was right about one thing: I am hurting again. To think I wouldn't be hurting was very naïve of me. In this life, hurt is inevitable.

I love someone. They break my heart. I pick up the pieces. Repeat.

I keep trusting. I keep being vulnerable. I keep getting hurt.

When will it stop? I just give up.

I throw my hands up on love. Love doesn't love anybody, especially me!

I fought the insecurity that Michael would cheat, and I won. I no longer believed that.

I fought the insecurity that he would abuse me. I won! I no longer believed that.

So when I let ALL my guards down, broke down all my walls, and I trusted him, I mean really trusted him, then I was told that I was not good enough.

My services were no longer desired.
Just dismissed!
Poof! Be gone. I give up. I surrender.
I am tired of crying.
I am tired of hurt.
I am tired of pain.
I am tired of sleepless nights.
I am tired of unhappiness.
I am tired. Just plain tired.
So where do I go from here?
Regroup?
I feel so lost, and I don't know what to do.
I am tired of trusting.
I am tired of loving.

It hurts too much and where is he? Sleeping.
Probably feeling a load has been lifted off of him. He
is finally free of me. Why can't I sleep? Well, cuz I'm
the one who's hurt.

In all of my relationships, I have never been
skinny enough, hard enough, sexy enough, clean
enough, smart enough, and timely enough.

I am NEVER enough.

So when they say they love you, do they really?

Love conquers all? Doesn't it?

Not in my case. That is because no one ever
truly loved me.

Love is patient. Love is kind. Love hopes in all
things and endures all things. Love never fails.

I seem to fail everyone...and everyone fails
me.

Spotlight on Recovery – Waiting Four Seasons:

It may be tempting to jump into the arms of another person when you flee one abusive relationship. Ideally, you should consider waiting at least one year (hence the "four seasons") for a number of reasons. You need to be able to heal completely from the trauma, realize that your new relationship is NOT your old relationship, and be able to gauge your readiness to begin again. If you start a relationship before you can mentally and emotionally process the realities of a new relationship, you can ruin a good one OR find yourself in another bad one. Before beginning a new relationship:

- **Seek counseling**. See a licensed clinician to begin to help you heal from your trauma and join a support group through your local domestic violence organization
- **Educate yourself**. Read every book, magazine, and online article you can get your hands on about the dynamics of abuse. Educate yourself on the characteristics of abuser and how and why he abuses will help you see your relationship from a different perspective.
- **Write a letter to God**. Pray to God and ask Him to direct your letter. Begin to write down all the things you'd like in a relationship. Write about EVERYTHING, including spiritual, physical, economic, and relationship characteristics. Then, put them in order from

most to least important. Take a look at your top ten (or top five). Those are non-negotiables. When you meet someone new, don't share the list. Use this as your measuring stick for whether or not this person should emerge as "the ONE."

- **Seek out other healthy relationships.** If you're like me, when you leave an abusive relationship, you may not have ever seen a healthy relationship. How can you HAVE what you've never experienced? Ask God to lead you to healthy couples to mentor you. You need to see a new "face" of relationships. Begin there.

- **Start a relationship with yourself.** You have spent the last few months, years, or decades catering to someone else. Do you even know WHO you are, WHAT you like to do, or WHERE you like to go? What is your favorite restaurant? Take yourself there. Don't know? Try a lot of them until you discover what it is. Take yourself to that movie you want to see. Go dancing. See that concert! All of the things you'd like to do with a partner, do by yourself. Learn to love yourself again.

What Can You Do About It?

Philippians 4:8-9 [8] Finally, brothers, whatever is true, whatever is honorable, whatever is just, whatever is pure, whatever is lovely, whatever is commendable, if there is any moral excellence and if there is any praise – dwell on these things. [9] Do what you have learned and received and heard and seen in me, and the God of peace will be with you.

How can you truly love someone else if you do not love yourself? Look at yourself in the mirror every day and begin to declare, "I am fearfully and wonderfully made. I am the apple of God's eyes. I am made in his image. I am beautiful. I am worthy of love." Focus on the wonderful things about you and allow God to change those parts of you that need to be changed. When you begin to see your worth, others will too.

Pray: Father God, teach me how to love myself in the way you love me. Teach me how to value my physical, intellectual, and spiritual assets. Help me to love myself. Show me that I never have to lower my standards in the name of having a relationship. Show me how to court myself and give me revelations of other healthy relationships. When the time comes, allow me to see and experience true love and not run away from it. In Jesus's name, Amen.

Chapter 23: From Velcro Girl to Teflon Girl

Diary Entry Wednesday, April 25, 2012

Dear Lord,

Right now, I'm feeling very overwhelmed by all of this stuff. Richard Read, the district attorney and Terrence's attorney, met with the judge in order to make a deal. I don't feel good about this.

Diary Entry Friday, April 27, 2012

Dear Lord,

On Monday I met with Richard Read about the possibility of Terrence pleading guilty. At the time, Terrence was ready to do so because all of his tests came back showing that he is fine; there is nothing mentally wrong with him. The judge offered him fifty years, and he was not happy with those terms. So on Wednesday, April 25, he went to court and pled not guilty.

But we now have to go to court (trial) the week of May 14. I was not happy at all.

I cried on and off all day at the prospect of that.

I don't want my children to have to go to court.

I don't want my business blasted on the news and then have to come back and face all the folks at school, Lord: parents, teachers, and other staff.

Lord, I wish all of this would go away. Please carry me through all of this. Please let justice be served for me, Corinne, and Theron. Please help us walk into the sunset, please. In Jesus's name!

Love,

Kimya

Margaret went to the hearing, and she said the judge acted as though he was not playing with Terrence. He asked for a continuance so that they could delay the case and seek medical care.

Margaret said the judge counted the months aloud all the way to April and said, "It's been seven months, and the family still hasn't had the medical testing done. Continuance denied..."

Then he tried to get sent back to the jail early by using his illness as an excuse, so he could leave the courtroom and wouldn't have to listen to the other inmates' stories.

The judge answered, "This man had been accused of shooting a woman and a child in the head. I am not giving him any special privileges. He can sit back there with the rest of them."

Then she said the judge called Terrence last.

Later that day... *It is now 3:00 on Friday afternoon, and I'm in the waiting area of the district attorney's office.*

Since we are going to have to go to trial, he wants to meet with me to discuss the specifics of the case. For once, I do not feel overly filled with anxiety.

Richard Read stated that Terrence wanted to have physical testing done, and the judge denied it. He still felt that Terrence would plead guilty, and he wanted me to bring the letter from the doctor about Terrence's sarcoidosis.

Diary Entry Sunday, April 29, 2012

Dear Lord,

Thank you for helping me make it through the Dirty Girl Run yesterday.

It was so, so scary going over that net, but as usual, you helped me make it through. I literally started crying when I got to the top. My coworker, Jackie, talked me over and even put my leg in the hole in the net so I could get across. I was so happy that my other coworkers, Jenee and Amy, went too. It was so much fun, and it was an incredible team-building experience. It would be great if we all could do it next year. Right after my meeting with the DA on Friday, it was just what I needed. I feel as if I have conquered something. Now I am sleepy and not feeling 100 percent, but Theron spent the night at Sandy's and...

(I fell asleep.)

May 2012

I was called in by Richard Read today. I was informed that Terrence has fired his attorney and hired a new one. We will not go to trial next week. I feel sick to my stomach.

289

If it weren't for other good news, I would be crazy somewhere. Mr. Read always does his best to help me feel secure with what's going on. He is such a patient and kind man, Lord. Thank You for assigning him to us.

On another note, words cannot express how grateful I am to You for the news I received today. I found out that Corinne passed her Criterion Reference Competency Test (CRCT).

June 2012

Dear Lord,

It has been very interesting in the last few weeks. I know that You wanted me to help women that are affected by domestic violence. I've known it ever since I was in the hospital. Women sought me out when I was there and told me how our story helped to bring them closer to Christ. One lady said that my story helped her to leave her abusive relationship. In the months leading up to now, I've heard "inspiration," "miracle," and "testimony" from the mouths of several people. So I knew that You would use me in an awesome way. I just figured that You wouldn't use me until I was totally healed.

Right now I am in the midst of appointments that include family therapy, individual counseling, and physical therapy. The trial hasn't even occurred, and I kept questioning how I could help anyone in the state I'm in. However, You have different plans for me.

*When I couldn't delay my destiny anymore, I decided to pull out my computer and email my pastor, Eric Lee, to tell him about my visions for the future. I just assumed that he would want me to **assist** with a domestic violence ministry.*

Imagine my surprise when he informed me that he wanted to partner with ME to "eradicate domestic violence in our community" and asked, "What should we do next?"

I looked at the computer in complete shock and disbelief and began shouting, "What do WE do next?! What do you mean by what do WE do next? I don't know what we do. I just want to help."

June 26, 2012

Hey Jehovah,

I had a really good session with Valerie today. I got some really good information. You just keep encouraging me to do more with this support group. She is going to hook me up with the person over the Task Force on Domestic Violence.

And You know I am going to this training on Thursday. After thinking and praying about what Pastor Lee told me, I found a domestic violence trainer in Illinois that teaches you how to run a Christian-based support group. Valerie feels like this will be a good step in my recovery.

Help me to make good contacts, Lord.

Help me to be able to go to dinner with people and not be lonely, Lord. I have never been anywhere by myself.

I want to focus on my healing and recovery too so I can help other people.

She said I could communicate with Michael through a letter and leave it at the house for him while I'm gone. I do value him. Of course we have arguments, and of course we have disagreements, but he is a good guy. I just don't think You're telling me to leave him.

She gave me a chapter title for my book: Velcro Girl and Teflon Girl. So, I'm going to make sure I put that in the book. It can show how I went from allowing everything people said and did to stick to me and hurt me to being able to discern the things that I should just be able to let go or roll off my back, so to speak. So, I'm excited Lord. I am excited about the changes You're making in my life. I am starting to feel much stronger. I am beginning to feel more empowered.

I love You, Lord, and I honor and cherish Your presence in my life. I LOVE YOU! And I will talk to You later, ok?

June 28, 2012

I arrived at the airport in Chicago without a hitch. I even called a taxi to bring me to the hotel, and I was not afraid at all.

This is the coolest room ever. I have a whole suite to myself. And it was supposed to cost more, but You gave me an awesome discount. Thank You for bringing me here safely. I am just in awe of this room.

Thank You, thank You, thank You. Love You. Bye!

June 29, 2012

Jehovah God, today was just so awesome! You've exceeded my expectations. You brought me here safely. You helped me to conquer my fears. I've made a lot of good contacts, and I'm sure I will make more tomorrow. Thank You for dinner at Pappadeaux with new friends.

And confirmation of what I should do.

You've given me lots of confirmation of Your will. I'm scared to do Your will, but I'm ready. I want to help other women win the war against domestic violence. Lord, please cover and protect me, my children, my sister, my dad, and my niece. Protect Michael.

Diary Entry Thursday, July 12, 2012

Dear Jehovah,

Thank you for all of Your comforting words this morning. I have chosen to forgive Terrence and his parents. I realize that his mom and dad love him as any parent would and fighting for his freedom is more about them, or just as much about them, as it is about him. By defending him, they are saying, "This is not the child we raised," and that some other entity has caused their son to act this way. I am sure they are hurt and embarrassed. It would break any parent's heart for this type of thing to happen to their child. I want to move on with my life and part of moving on means that I have to forgive them. I am ready and willing. Please continue to help my heart and the hearts of my children, family, and friends.

Love, Kimya

Diary Entry Thursday, July 26, 2012

Dear Jehovah,

The last two days have been two of the hardest days I've had to encounter in the past year.

Tuesday night, after I had a great open house at school, I got a call from the nursing home where daddy is staying. They said my dad is in the hospital, and then I got the shock of my life; they said my daddy would not make it.

By the time I got there, he died four times and was resuscitated. I told them he had a "do not resuscitate" order in place. He told me when we completed his living will that he never wanted to be placed on any machines and he didn't want to be resuscitated. I feel like I failed Daddy because they put his body through so much trauma.

I walked over to his bedside, sat down in the chair next to him, and laid my head on his bed. I grabbed daddy's hands and started rubbing his arm.

"Daddy, I love you so much." I wasn't sure if he could hear me, but his eyes were partially open. "Daddy, I am so sorry they hooked you up to that machine four times. I know it hurt you. I told them that you didn't want that to happen."

Tears started rolling down my cheeks, and I continued to talk to him while the heart monitor beeped to my every word.

"Daddy? "He took a deep breath, but he didn't respond. Still, that made me believe he could hear and understand me. I went on telling him about all the fun times we had together when I was a child. I told him how much Sandy and I loved him. I told him how much the children loved him. I didn't tell him anything about the abuse from the past. I wanted him to have nothing but happy thoughts in his head.

I got up from the chair, kissed him on the forehead, and left the room.

Sandy went in to speak to him a little bit, and she came out quickly.

We left the hospital and received a call around 4 a.m. Daddy died.

Diary Entry Wednesday, August 16, 2012

Dear Jehovah,

I think it is official. I am depressed again. Starting school, daddy dying, planning his funeral, being a mom, and being a girlfriend has been too much for me, and I feel as if I am about to explode. I feel so weakened...so hurt...so lost.

Diary Entry Sunday, August 26, 2012

Dear Jehovah God,

You are so AWESOME! I cannot think of any word to describe Your complete and total awesomeness, but You are making me feel pretty awesome right now. Just two weeks after daddy's death, Michael totally surprised me.

Yesterday was one of the happiest days of my life. It is a moment that will be forever placed in my memory. We went to dinner at Los Charros yesterday to celebrate me and Sandy's birthday. We were really taking her out because she is turning fifty on Tuesday, and I will be thirty-nine.

But nevertheless, after dinner and a pitcher of daiquiris, Michael reminded Sandy and me that we had to exchange presents.

So after we finished, he said, "It's my turn now, right?" He scooted his chair away from mine and got down on his knees.

"Ms. Motley, we've gone through so much together. We've been through so many ups and downs, but guess what? I wouldn't trade it for anything in the world. I love you and your kids. Will you marry me?

I started crying and said, "Yes!"

Of course I said yes!

He gave me my moment and a special story to tell forever. I will always love him for that. No one has ever proposed to me before. I always wanted that, and HE gave it to me. Michael Langley is one special man! Thank You, Lord, for him.

Thank You, Jesus!

Love always and forever,

Kimya

Spotlight on Recovery – Forgiveness:

Unforgiveness imprisons your heart in a cage of bitterness and resentment. If you do not forgive, you will walk around with so much weight on your shoulders and the only one feeling down and depressed all of the time is YOU. The perpetrator of the "crime" has probably gone on with his life. On top of that, harboring unforgiveness can have an effect on your mental and physical health. According to the docs at St. Hopkins, harboring resentment puts you in chronic fight or flight mode, which could mean changes in blood pressure, inconsistencies in immune response, and fluctuations in heart rates, which increase your risk for heart disease, depression, post-traumatic stress disorder, and diabetes. Who needs that?! The benefits of forgiveness are much better. How about lowering your cholesterol and risk of heart attack; improving your sleep; and lessening symptoms of depression, anxiety, and stress? ("Forgiveness," n.d.)
So, how do you forgive?

- **Make the decision.** Just decide you want to forgive the person.
- **Write a letter.** Write a letter to the person you need to forgive. Tell him all of the things they did to hurt you. Get it all out! Then, in the letter, express your forgiveness. You don't have to actually send the letter (or you can if you need to do so). If you choose NOT to send it, tear up the letter in little pieces or burn it.
- **Free yourself.** Come to the realization that the person chose not to love you in the way

you deserved or desired. They gave you all they were capable of giving and you deserve better than they were willing to offer.

- **Forgive yourself.** Fast from regret. The past happened and there is nothing you can do about it. The best thing about it is learning whatever lesson this situation gave you and moving on. Regret only punishes you and holds you in a holding pattern of bondage.

What can you do about it?

Matthew 18:21-22 [21]Then Peter came to Him and said, "Lord, how many times could my brother sin against me and I forgive him? As many as seven times?" [22]"I tell you, not as many as seven," Jesus said to him, "but 70 times seven."

Pray and ask the Lord to help you forgive the person who hurt you. Every time feelings of hurt, regret, and/or resentment surfaces, pray and ask God to help you to forgive. I believe Jesus is not telling Peter to give someone 490 opportunities to hurt him; it means you may have to pray and ask for help with this 490 times until you can truly forgive. Every time a negative thought pops up about the person, pray and ask God to help you forgive. Next, start praying for the perpetrator (i.e. his needs, desires, and for a change of heart). Before you know it, you are basking in the glow of forgiveness.

Pray: Father God, teach me how to forgive others in the way that you forgive me. Remove all bitterness, hatred, and enmity from my heart. I pray for the person who wronged me. Forgive them of their sins. Create in us both a clean heart and renew in us a right spirit. Help _____ to see the error of his ways. Help me to walk in forgiveness. In Jesus' name, Amen.

Chapter 24: The Trial

Diary entry: October 26, 2012

Dear Lord,

'Twas the day of the sentencing, when all through the house not a creature was stirring, except me and Peanut. I've been up since about 5 a.m. trying to get it together for the sentencing that is going to take place at 10:00 a.m. today. For some reason, I'm not fearful. Thank You, Holy Spirit, for that.

What I kind of feel is empty and detached— almost like I'm going to a funeral. One thing for sure is that I am no longer afraid of him. I pray and ask You that my children are able to reach that point as well.

Jehovah God, by the power of your Holy Spirit and in the name of Jesus, please let a spirit of peace fall afresh over everyone in attendance today in our courtroom.

Send forth all of your warring angels to force out and keep out all demonic spirits and forces of darkness from everywhere we are, everywhere we are going, and everywhere we will be. Do not allow them to manifest, follow, attack, or oppress anyone today and into tonight and all the days of our lives.

Please allow your virtue, truth, peace, and, most of all, justice rule and reign inside this courtroom today, over my home, and over everyone connected to this in anyway. Please allow all these things that have happened to us to be turned around for my family's EVERLASTING good!

Now unto Him (that's You) who is able to do exceedingly and abundantly more than I can ask, think, or imagine. Do Your thing, Lord J! Please let this morning and this whole weekend go smoothly. Use me Lord as your mouthpiece on the Earth today. Touch the hearts, minds, courage, will, and determination of others. Heal families today. Amen.

8:00 a.m.

Trying to get Theron and Corinne dressed wasn't as hard as I believed it would be. They were too excited about getting to miss school that they were not thinking about the impact of what was about to happen.

"Mom, are we going to get something delicious after this thing? Cuz I am kinda hungry."

Theron was always hungry.

"Yes, baby. Can we talk about that when we leave?"

302

He continued to talk about all the types of "deliciousness" he could eat as we drove toward the courthouse. My mind drifted off to the words I needed to say.

How would I feel when I saw him? Sad? Angry? Vengeful?

What would he say or do?

Would he say he was sorry to me? Corinne?

Would he try to defend his actions?

I found comfort that his body was taped with several thousand volts of electricity, and if he even tried anything, they would light his butt up. I was ready to face him. I would NOT be fearful.

Turning right onto Milstead, I finally saw that three-story, brick building. It was beautifully adorned with tall, white columns. "**ROCKDALE COUNTY COURTHOUSE**" was prominently displayed in huge, white letters outside the building. I knew that my life would change, and the lives of others would be affected by what went on inside that building that morning.

Finding a parking spot was easy; getting out of the car to walk to the building was not. I took several deep breaths to try to steady my wobbling knees and hoped my heart, which was beating as fast as a racehorse at this point, would slow down.

"Help me, Holy Spirit," I whispered under my breath.

We passed several black families out in the parking lot. I couldn't help but wonder if any of them were there to support Terrence.

Were they mad with me?

Would they try to hurt me?

Would they say something mean to me?

Where was his mom? His dad?

I quickly dismissed any feelings of fear. I WAS ready to do this.

I HAD to do this.

Walking to our seats past rows and rows of rich mahogany pews (like a church) in that courtroom seemed almost surreal. A million thoughts seemed to be crowding my mind at the time. Although I had many supporters there with me, they could not drown out the sounds in my head.

How would I react when I saw him?

How would Corinne and Theron react?

Corinne sat next to Sandy and Courtney in the courtroom. I could tell my baby was afraid. She kept biting her nails and turning to watch the entrance.

As Terrence was escorted into the courtroom in his orange jump suit and with chains around his arms and feet, the courtroom grew quiet.

Corinne began to cry, and my sister kind of rocked her.

We sat through his mom, former co-workers, and friends, giving positive testimony about him. Even the sheriff of the county where Terrence was from sent in a letter talking about how wonderful Terrence was.

Then it was my turn.

With tears streaming down my face, I read:

"I cannot begin to explain how deeply painful and emotionally challenging this past year has been. For myself, I endured one of the worst emotional and physical pains imaginable.

Terrence ambushed Corinne and me that dark and drizzly morning on September 20th while I dropped her off at the daycare center. As she walked to go to the ramp to put her shoe on, he rounded the back of my car, startling me, and shouted, 'I told you I was going to kill your ass, didn't I?' while simultaneously shooting me in the face. That bullet pierced my face with the heat of a thousand fires and delivered a blow strong enough to shatter the left side of my jaw, causing me to have to endure surgery, five months of having my mouth wired shut, and extensive physical therapy, which continues up to this very day."

Up until this point, I was looking down at my paper. I was too afraid to look at him. But all of a sudden, it was as if a surge of fearlessness or the Holy Spirit Himself took over me, and I looked up. Right into his face. Eye to eye. He sat there with a blank, expressionless look on his face. There was no emotion at all. Just emptiness. I continued reading.

"The next shot was delivered to the left side of my neck as I attempted to run away from him. I was filled with terror for my life, and, not knowing where Corinne was in all of this, I was more concerned that she would witness her mother dying in front of her. The thought never even crossed my mind that he would shoot her, too.

I quickly discovered that I couldn't run at all and collapsed on the ground just a short distance away. Terrence stood over me, execution style, and as I wildly began to shake my head back and forth on the ground, he shot me in the back of the head.

Several shots later, we were made it into the childcare center to get help. We were taken into another room in the daycare center because the child in the adjacent room was watching us. The 911 operator must have instructed the teacher to put Corinne on the floor and get some towels because we were bleeding so extensively.

I had to watch Corinne slip in and out of consciousness. I had to watch Corinne vomit blood and bile. I would shake her and scream her name because I didn't want her to die.

I started praying out loud, 'Holy Spirit, please don't let him take my baby from me.' At that point, the ambulance and helicopter arrived, and, despite my protests, they separated us."

I recounted the events of the morning as if I were right there, experiencing them all over again. His face remained like a rock, unmovable. I thought after hearing what he did to Corinne, Terrence would begin to show some emotion. He did not.

At that point, I could no longer contain the tears and emotion that I kept bottled up until that moment. Hot tears flooded my face, but somehow my voice became stronger.

"Terrence has no idea the magnitude of the damage he caused by the choices he made that day. I am not sure what hurt me the most.

Could it be the day when he shot Corinne and I had to watch my daughter fight for her life?

Could it be the day that Dr. Chern told her grandmother, father, and my aunt that she would not make it?

Could it be the first day I saw her when she was hooked up to every machine imaginable to help her eat and maintain brain pressure? She had tubes and wires that were connected from machines that whirred and buzzed to what seemed like every square inch of her body.

Maybe it was the weeks when I watched her learn how to eat, walk, and talk all over again.

No, I would say it was one day in November, shortly after she had been released from the hospital after five weeks of intense rehabilitation.

She was crying and rocking in pain from the excruciating headache that was ravaging her body when she yelled at me, 'Somebody better tell me who did this to me! Mommy, who did this to me?'"

I looked him dead in his eyes. There was still no emotion.

"When I told her that it was Terrence that shot her in the head, the look of betrayal and hurt in her eyes was immeasurable. She cried and held me so tightly as she asked me repeatedly, 'Why did he do this to me? Was I a bad child? Did he really hate me? I thought he loved me, Mommy.'

These questions were asked to me repeatedly over the past year. She loved Terrence so much, and even though he wasn't her biological father, she told everyone that he was her dad. I remember just a few weeks before the shooting, Terrence asked me if after we divorced, would I take Corinne away from him, too? I asked Corinne if she still wanted him to be her dad, and she said, "Yes." She didn't care that we were getting divorced. In her eyes, Terrence would always be her dad."

My words became more intense and angry I looked for a hint of remorse, a hint of regret, a hint that he loved this child that wanted so desperately for him to be her dad.

But there was still nothing.

"Corinne had always excelled in math before the shooting, and now she struggles. Today, Corinne is in special education classes. She cries and talks about how she feels as if she is not smart and learning is much more difficult for her now. Being an athletic person, she has not been able to participate in the sports she loves or even something as simple as elementary school P.E. courses. Corinne's self-esteem is suffering as well because every week she has to endure the teasing of classmates because of her scar on the side of her head. She was asked if she were a boy because her hair was so short due to two brain surgeries and was questioned by well-meaning children: 'Hey, aren't you the one that was shot?' She simply wishes she could just be a 'normal' child.

To top that off, she has suffered the loss of the one man she had learned to love and trust. Terrence has hurt her much more emotionally than he ever could have done physically. And while the physical scars have healed on the outside, on the inside, she wages a daily battle with her ability to learn, love, and trust again."

At this point, I couldn't stand to look at him any longer. My eyes went back to my paper, and I prayed that no hatred and bitterness would take hold in my heart. I took a deep breath and asked the Holy Spirit to help me read the final portion of my letter.

"It is not my job to judge a person because the Bible says that only God can judge Terrence. However, if I were given a say in the matter, I would request that Terrence receive the maximum sentence allowable. Terrence is an angry man that made some poor choices in his health, business, and our marriage. The choices he made caused his life to spiral out of control. While he appeared to be a wonderful and helpful friend to everyone on the outside, he was very violent and controlling to my son and me. As long as his home-maintenance business was successful, he was a kind and loving husband. However, whenever he mismanaged money, got ill from cigarette-induced bouts of sarcoidosis, headaches, colds, or when customers did not pay him as expected, he became cold, distant, angry, and violent toward Theron and me. This began in 2008 and continued up until the day he shot Corinne and me.

Through the years, he has threatened me with cyanide poisoning, antifreeze poisoning, and hurting me in public. Terrence was removed from our home, and he's pled guilty to physically assaulting my son in 2010 simply because Theron begged him to please not hit his Mommy again. When I asked him why he would discipline Theron so harshly, he would tell me that he was raised that way. When I begged him to get counseling for himself and our family, he contended that there was nothing wrong with him. He said that counseling doesn't help anyone, and it wasn't going to change a damn thing. Terrence is the same person that told me that this is who he was and he wasn't going to change. He told me that he wasn't going to give me a divorce and that the only way we would part would be through death."

I found a deeper determination within in me to look up one last time. This time, I looked at the faces of all of my supporters: my family, my friends, the judge, Amanda, Mr. Read, and even Terrence's family.

My eyes found Corinne and Theron, and my heart connected to the pain they must be experiencing. Corinne cried as I read the impact statement, and my aunt whispered something in Theron's ears, which appeared to calm him down. I knew I had to finish strong.

"In conclusion, this incident will forever leave an indelible mark, not only on Corinne and myself, but on my son (who had to be hospitalized for major depression after the incident), our family, our friends, Terrence's family, the children in the daycare that witnessed the incident, and the community at large who reached out to us in our time of need.

Corinne and I look great on the outside, and thanks to the grace of God and weeks of intensive individual and family counseling, we are striving day by day to reach a point of mental and emotional well-being.

No one should have to endure what we've had to endure, and I want Judge Nation and the people of Rockdale County to ensure that no one else will suffer at the hands of Terrence.

There are intervention programs offered by the county to help the offenders and counseling services for their families; however, when the offenders do not accept the help that is given, they will have to endure the consequences of their actions.

Judge Nation, since Terrence did not seek the help that was offered to him, when he began abusing us, I am asking that you set precedence in this case. I do not want another man in Rockdale County to think he can do this to his wife and child and get away with it."

And with that, I got up from the stand and went back to my seat.

Judge Nation called Terrence to the stand and asked him if he had any last words. He shook his head and uttered a simple "No."

His attorney said, "My client would like to enter a plea of guilty."

Judge Sidney Nations sentenced him to sixty-five years with 50 to serve.

Afterword

Dear Reader,

My life since the shooting has been filled with many highs and lows, but the important thing is that I keep going because I get my strength from God.

My relationship with Michael ended one year after the sentencing. He was very supportive to my children and me during our time of tragedy and what happened afterward. The shooting forever changed my life and the person that I was. The emotional and spiritual changes I underwent were difficult for me, and I am sure they were for him as well. He has since moved on and has gotten married to a wonderful woman.

As of the date of publication, my son has completed three years of college and is working part-time at a job he loves.

My daughter triumphs in sports! In sixth grade, she ran track and went to the State Finals, where she was ranked ninth in the state for her event. Corinne played basketball for her middle school in eighth grade, and after NEVER playing soccer a day in her life, she made the JV team in tenth grade and played some varsity games as well.

We have all returned to family counseling, which is great and helpful in the rebuilding process. Domestic violence can have long-reaching effects on children. The good news is that children are incredibly resilient and can overcome the effects when they have God in their lives, a strong, caring adult who is willing to tell them how much they are loved and that the abuse is not their fault, and a licensed counselor to help them deal with overwhelming feelings of anger, depression, grief, and loss.

I have founded an organization called Haven of Light International. We help women, children, AND men (yes, men!) overcome domestic violence. I travel all over Georgia doing speaking events to educate the community and recruit "soldiers" to fight against the violence against women.

I hope this book has taught you that you don't have to be a victim of someone else's anger; you do have a choice. The process of leaving and starting over will not be easy, but it will be worth it. At times you will doubt your sanity, strength, and support system, but you can have better relationships and you don't have to settle for less.. Ever.

God is definitely in the miracle-making business. Even with our imperfections, God is still full of grace and mercy. I was born into a home filled with domestic violence. The neighborhoods that I grew up in were filled with sexual horrors. My teenage and young adult relationships included one abusive situation after the next. These facts meant that I was doomed to a life of depression and dysfunctional relationships. That was all true.

But with God, I overcame domestic and sexual violence. This means I am resilient, confident, and strong. I am an overcomer!

While negative things in my life were born of violence, positive things were born of violence, too. Had the shooting never occurred, I would not have become an advocate for women battling domestic violence and you would not be reading this book. I pray this book will help you or others you know that are faced with the horrors of domestic violence.

My dear reader, if my family and I can overcome our obstacles and begin to rebuild our lives, you can, too. No matter what has happened to you, your past should not hinder your future. Even if you have not faced domestic violence, but you are facing some other tragedy or you are trying to rebuild your life after loss, I pinkie promise you can persevere through it. We all have obstacles to overcome and with God as the CEO of your life, you can't fail. Allow Him to turn your tragedy into triumph!

Love,

Kimya

Author's Bio

Ms. Kimya N. Motley is a certified educator and instructional coach with over twenty years of teaching experience in Georgia Public Schools, including DeKalb, Rockdale, and Gwinnett counties.

She received a Bachelor of Sciences in a dual program with the College of Family and Consumer Sciences and the College of Education from the University of Georgia. She also received a Masters of Sciences in Counseling Psychology from The University of Missouri.

Motley earned the distinction of Teacher of the Year for Rosebud Elementary and has served on the Teacher Advisory Council to the Gwinnett County School System's Superintendent during the 2015-2016 school year. In recognition for her work as an educator, she has received commendations from Kelly Kautz, Mayor of Snellville, and State Senator Gloria Butler.

After surviving a tragedy in 2011, in which Motley's ex-husband ambushed her at a daycare center and shot her and her daughter in the head, Motley founded Haven of Light International, Inc. in May 2013.

Haven of Light International is a non-profit designed to help families rebuild spiritually, physically, emotionally, and financially after abuse.

In addition to helping families through Haven of Light, Motley is an inspirational speaker for organizations and events in support of fighting domestic violence, teen dating violence, and sex trafficking. She received a commendation from Governor Deal in March 2016 for her work as a leading domestic violence advocate. The Investigation Discovery Channel named her their Everyday Hero in November 2016 for the work she does inspiring a difference in the lives of others through her dedication to victims' rights and healing.

Motley enjoys reading; dining out; pinning recipes to her Pinterest board (that she wishes she had more time to make); and spending time with her son, Theron, her daughter, Corinne, and her Pomeranian, Peanut

Booking information:

Website: KimyaMotley.com
Havenoflightint.org
Email: info@KimyaMotley.com
Kimya@havenoflightint.org
Social Media:. Facebook, Instagram, Twitter, YouTube, LinkedIn @KimyaMotley

References

50 Obstacles to Leaving: 1 - 10. (n.d.). Retrieved from
http://www.thehotline.org/2013/06/10/50-
obstacles-to-leaving-1-10/

Adult Survivors of Child Sexual Abuse. (n.d.) Retrieved
from https://www.rainn.org/articles/adult-survivors-
child-sexual-abuse

Cohen, L. R., Field, C., Campbell, A. N. C., & Hien, D. A.
(2013). Intimate Partner Violence Outcomes in
Women with PTSD and Substance Use: A Secondary
Analysis of NIDA Clinical Trials Network "Women
and Trauma" Multi-Site Study. Addictive Behaviors,
38(7), 2325–2332.
http://doi.org/10.1016/j.addbeh.2013.03.006

Crabtree-Nelson, S.V. (2010). How Counseling Helps: An
In-Depth Look at Domestic Violence Counseling.
Retrieved from
http://ecommons.luc.edu/cgi/viewcontent.cgi?article=
1262&context=luc_diss

Cycle of Violence. (n.d.). Retrieved from
https://www.dvsac.org/cycles-of-violence/

Domestic Violence: Orders of Protection and Restraining
Orders. (n.d.). Retrieved from
http://family.findlaw.com/domestic-violence/domestic-
violence-orders-of-protection-and-restraining-
orders.html

Facts about Domestic Violence and Economic Abuse (2015)
Retrieved from
https://ncadv.org/assets/2497/domestic_violence_and_
economic_abuse_ncadv.pdf

Facts About Domestic Violence and Stalking. (2015).
Retrieved from
https://ncadv.org/assets/2497/domestic_violence_and_
stalking_ncadv.pdf

Finding Closure After Abuse. (2013, May 14). Retrieved
From http://www.thehotline.org/2013/05/14/finding-
closure-after-abuse/

Forgiveness: Your Health Depends On It. (n.d.). Retrieved
from
http://www.hopkinsmedicine.org/health/healthy_agin
g/healthy_connections/forgiveness-your-health-
depends-on-it

Grovert, A.J. (2008, July 7). Domestic Violence Against
Women: A Literature Review. Retrieved from
http://commons.pacificu.edu/cgi/viewcontent.cgi?artic
le=1037&context=spp

How Police are Trained to Respond to Domestic
Violence. (n.d.). Retrieved from
https://www.domesticshelters.org/domestic-violence-
articles-information/how-police-are-trained-to-
respond-to-domestic-violence#.Wd7oRxjMy9Y

Red Flags of Abuse (n.d.) Retrieved from
https://nnedv.org/content/red-flags-of-abuse/

What is Spiritual Abuse. (2015, November 12). Retrieved
Retrieved from
http://www.thehotline.org/2015/11/12/what-is-
spiritual-abbuse/

When Your Support System Isn't Clear. (n.d.). Retrieved
From https://www.domesticshelters.org/domestic-
violence-articles-information/when-your-support-
system-isn-t-clear#.WeHtmxjMzBJ